Brigadier General States Rights Gist,
Provisional Army of the Confederate States.
(South Carolina Confederate Relic Room and Museum)

STATES RIGHTS GIST

A South Carolina General
Of The Civil War

BY

WALTER BRIAN CISCO

 WHITE MANE PUBLISHING COMPANY, INC.

This White Mane Publishing Company, Inc. publication
was printed by
Beidel Printing House, Inc.
63 West Burd Street
Shippensburg, PA 17257

In respect for the scholarship contained herein, the acid-free paper used in this book meets the guidelines for permanence and durability of the Committee on Production Guidelines for Book Longevity of the Council on Library Resources.

For a complete list of available publications
please write
White Mane Publishing Company, Inc.
P. O. Box 152
Shippensburg, PA 17257

Library of Congress Cataloging-in-Publication Data

Cisco, Walter Brian, 1947-
    States Rights Gist : a South Carolina general of the Civil War / by Walter Brian Cisco.
        p.   cm.
    Includes bibliographical references and index.
    ISBN 0-942597-28-1. -- ISBN 0-942597-29-X (limited edition)
        1. Gist, States Rights, 1831 -   .   2. Generals--Confederate States of America--Biography.   3. Confederate States of America. Army--Biography.   4. South Carolina--History--Civil War, 1861-1865.
    I. Title.
    E467.1.G45C57   1991
    973.7'3'092--dc20
    [B]
                                                        91-30467
                                                        CIP

PRINTED IN THE UNITED STATES OF AMERICA

Table of Contents

1. "Scarce Had Wyoming of War or Crime Heard" 1

2. "The World is the Battle Ground" 14

3. "Nodding Plumes and Brilliant Uniforms" 30

4. "No Flag But the Palmetto" 38

5. "Young Men Are Dying to Fight For It" 48

6. "I Knowed He Was a General" 60

7. "He is the Junior and Obeys Orders Only" 73

8. "Sanctify Yourselves Against To Morrow" 89

9. "Gist's Brigade is Just Coming Up" 97

10. "The Finest One in This Army" 115

11. "I Might Get Tripped Up This Evening" 132

Epilogue 146

Appendix 1   The Death of General Gist 152

Appendix 2   The Staff of States Rights Gist 154

Notes 156

Bibliography 185

Index 194

List of Maps

Confederate Defenses of
 Charleston, South Carolina 76

The Battle of Chickamauga 99

The Atlanta Campaign 113

The Battle of Franklin 137

Acknowledgments

People will go out of their way to be helpful. At every step in the research and writing of this book I have encountered courtesy and support for which I am grateful.

Especially am I indebted to the knowledgeable and patient staffs of the University of South Carolina's South Caroliniana Library, the Thomas Cooper Library, the University of South Carolina Archives, the South Carolina Department of Archives and History, the Union County Library, Duke University's William R. Perkins Library, the University of North Carolina's Southern Historical Collection and the Library of Congress.

A host of individuals have aided me with their expertise, guidance or simple encouragement. I offer my sincere thanks to: Mike Raines, Harvard University Archives; Judith W. Mellins, Harvard Law School Library; Jane M. Yates, the Citadel Archives; John M. Bigham, South Carolina Confederate Relic Room and Museum; Chris Hightower and Renae Farris of Rose Hill Plantation State Park; Dr. Allan D. Charles, University of South Carolina at Union; Dr. Walter B. Edgar, Director of the University of South Carolina's Institute for Southern Studies; Cory Hudgins, Museum of the Confederacy; Ronald T. Clemmons; Dr. Daniel Walker Hollis; Laura J. Hopkins; John A. Biggerstaff, Jr.; L.C. Hickman; A. Mason Gibbes; J.H. Brooks; Mrs. John W. Walker; Dr. John F. Brown; Jessamine D. Gist; Gene Jones; and my brother, David Cisco.

Walter Brian Cisco

Cordova, South Carolina

For Amanda and Steven

Chapter One
"Scarce Had Wyoming of War or Crime Heard"

Across the hills and fields twenty thousand steel bayonets gleamed in the late afternoon sun, divided at intervals by a hundred crimson banners. Bands played bravely to the accompaniment of exploding shells, shouted orders, and the nervous neighing of horses. Their ranks stretching two miles, the combat-hardened veterans of the Rebel Army of Tennessee lined up as if on parade. In a moment they would surge forward against Yankee-fortified Franklin in one more desperate struggle to keep alive the dream of Southern independence.

In the front line, bracing his men for the assault, was Brigadier General States Rights Gist, Provisional Army of the Confederate States. The South Carolinians and Georgians revered their handsome young general with the unforgettable name. Astride his charger, waving his hat as he galloped up and down the line, he presented the perfect picture of martial glory. Once more he would lead his command into battle, proud of their gallant record and confident of victory.

That night, in far-away South Carolina, the Gist family gathered to watch at the deathbed of the General's brother,

1

Nathaniel. Disability had kept the middle-aged planter from service in his country's army. Ironically he had contracted typhoid while on a mournful journey to the front to retrieve the remains of a dead relative. Now as he lay at home delirious with fever, his sister Sarah tried to calm the sufferer.

"Sarah, States was killed this afternoon leading his troops in battle."

Everyone in the room strained to catch Nathaniel's words. There had been no bad news since the army headed toward Tennessee.

"No, brother," gently replied Sarah, "States is all right — you were just dreaming."

Her soothing was useless. Inexplicably, the fever-ravaged Nathaniel had seen something and refused to be comforted. "I know that States is dead," he pronounced with finality.[1]

The story of the Gist* family in South Carolina began with the arrival of young William Gist on the eve of the Revolutionary War. He had chosen a land of contrast. Already Charles Town was nearing her centennial, proud citadel of tradition and elegant living; the crowded cobblestone streets and busy docks ruled by the bells of St. Michael's Church. Yet in the stillness of William's frontier world, the great city seemed as distant as his native Maryland. South Carolina's interior was part of a vast continental wilderness that coastal tidewater civilization had long been reluctant to penetrate. Emboldened by news of peace with the Cherokees, immigrants from Pennsylvania, Maryland and Virginia trooped to the red hills and pine forests of the upcountry. William joined the exodus, and near the banks of the Tyger River in what would become Union District, determined to make a home.[2]

The Gist family had been in America at least ninety years. Records show English-born Christopher Gist (or Guest) living in Baltimore in 1682. He took for a wife Edith

*"Gist" is pronounced with a hard G.

Cromwell, a distant kinswoman of the Lord Protector. Their only son Richard lived a respectable life as surveyor and militia captain.[3]

A practical man like William would have no inclination to dwell on the past or venerate ancestors he never knew. But if anyone could inspire him, it would be his Uncle Christopher. Well-known frontiersman, guide and soldier, Christopher Gist explored a wide area of the Ohio Valley. He was a friend of the young Major George Washington and is said to have twice saved the future President's life. "Washington was to find Gist capable of handling both compass and canoe, a man altogether conscientious in the performance of duty," acknowledged the President's biographer, Douglas Southall Freeman.[4]

William likely was also acquainted with the exploits of cousin Nathaniel Gist, Christopher's son. He could scarcely avoid hearing the gossip. While trading with the Indians in Tennessee, Nathaniel fathered a child by a part-Cherokee girl. Illegitimate birth and mixed blood did not cripple the boy. First called George Gist, the enigmatic genius became a devoted educator and inventor of the Cherokee alphabet. History would know him as Sequoyah.[5]

There was no time for waywardness in William's routine. Hard work brought prosperity, and now in his early thirties he was thinking of marriage. Perhaps it was the businesslike and dependable nature of Sarah Fincher that attracted his attention. She was born in Pennsylvania and migrated south with her family when still a young girl. William and Sarah were married about 1774 and over the next seven years had five sons.

Agitation for colonial rights, and eventually American independence, seemed only treason to this farmer. Described as "a man of substance" with "great landed property," he risked everything in stubborn loyalty to the Crown. When hostilities began in 1776, his active support of the Tory cause landed him for a time in a Charles Town prison. Later he served as a captain of South Carolina Loyalists and fought at the battle of King's Mountain. During the course of the war he was captured twice, escaped both times and was forced to hide in the woods for many months. With the British defeat, he fled to safety in England, leaving his family in the care of Sarah's parents.

At first their land was confiscated and part sold. Later the state returned five hundred acres to Sarah Gist, making it possible for her to move back into her own home and enter the mercantile business. Her wholesale supplier was none other than her husband in England. While he remained in exile, she built this enterprise and increased the family's land holdings in Union District, all in her own name. By 1789 William Gist felt confident in returning to South Carolina. The family made Charleston* their new home, continuing as merchants in the city but retaining their country property.[6]

Post-war Charleston was the place chosen for retirement by Mordecai Gist. Another cousin, he and William Gist were born in Maryland the same year but ended up on opposite sides of what was truly America's first civil war. While William suffered privation and persecution for his Tory sympathies, Mordecai Gist rose rapidly in the ranks of the patriot army. The battles of Long Island, Germantown, and Camden added luster to his name. He had earned a brigadier general's commission in 1779. Mordecai Gist's single-minded if not flamboyant patriotism was reflected in the naming of his two sons. The first he called Independent, the second was christened States.[7]

William Gist never returned to the Tyger River. He died in Charleston in 1802 and was buried in St. Michael's churchyard, also the resting place of his cousin the general. William had outlived Sarah by six years. In his will he made provision for each of their children, but the bulk of the estate, including the Charleston business and eight slaves, he left to sons Nathaniel and Francis.[8]

Nathaniel was born in 1776 on the Gist country homestead. With the family separated by war, imprisonment and

---

*"Charles Town" officially became "Charleston" in 1783.

exile, he was a teenager before ever really knowing his father. They were much alike in their business sense, desire to succeed, and tenacious adherence to principle. But, while William had abandoned his youthful ambition of living on the land, his son took up the challenge. Even as the business on King Street prospered, Nathaniel dreamed of one day leaving the congested metropolis and embracing again the rural life he remembered as a boy. As the years passed, and opportunity arose, he purchased land near Fair Forest Creek, a tributary of the Tyger River, a site well-known for its verdant beauty. In 1811 two grants from the state pushed his holdings to over three thousand acres. The long sojourn was over. He departed to the red hills of his birth.[9]

Now a substantial landowner and already thirty-five, Nathaniel Gist longed for marriage and a family of his own. The young lady he courted and won was a neighbor's daughter, Elizabeth McDaniel, fifteen years his junior. She was an impulsive young woman; her strong emotions tempered by the propriety of a good Presbyterian upbringing. There was a simple, unpretentious way about her that earned the trust of others and somehow made her profession of faith in Christ all the more genuine. "She was pleasant," remembered one friend, "because it seemed impossible for her to be otherwise."[10]

During those years Nathaniel Gist built a reputation in the community as one who never turned the other cheek, a man stubbornly jealous of his rights. Some thought him downright contentious. On a Sabbath day in June 1814 he angrily confronted one Andrew McBride Thompson who was trespassing and probably drunk. A few days later Gist wrote Colonel Hugh Means describing the incident, denigrating Thompson's character and claiming the intruder's purpose had been to "commence a riot." Thompson in turn sued the letter writer for libel in Court of General Sessions, calling Gist "a person of envious, evil and wicked mind and a most malicious disposition..." The case was thrown out of court in October 1815.[11] Two years later the vigilant landowner

Nathaniel Gist, father of
States Rights Gist.
*(From Wilson Gee,
The Gist Family)*

Elizabeth Lewis McDaniel
Gist, General Gist's
mother. "Her pleasantry
was the genuine article,
nothing caustic, nothing
bitter."
*(From Wilson Gee,
The Gist Family)*

apprehended an armed party on his property and assaulted their leader. Unfortunately for Gist, the victim was Captain Charles Cunningham of a militia squad "then being in the actual performance of patrol duty in the service of God and the State..." This time the court found him guilty.[12] As Gist entered middle age, a man of wealth and responsibility, the petty, personal incidents finally ceased. In years to come his proclivity for "righting wrongs" would seek a larger, political context.

No one is sure just why Gist called his new home Wyoming. Family tradition has the name coming from Scotsman Thomas Campbell's poem "Gertrude of Wyoming," published in 1809. The beautiful if tragic story is set in the Wyoming Valley of Pennsylvania and tells of the devastation wrought in the War for Independence. Nathaniel Gist may have been inspired by the poem's idyllic picture of ordered peace, a security he missed as a child and was now determined to enjoy.

> *And scarce had Wyoming of war or crime*
> *Heard, but in transatlantic story rung,*
> *For here the exile met from every clime,*
> *And spoke in friendship every distant tongue;*[13]

Wyoming was fashioned with lumber cut from the heart of the ancient pines.[14] Copying the custom of Charleston, the two stories were elevated on a raised brick basement. The house would retain a simple dignity, even as it was expanded and remodeled over the years. Downstairs were four high-ceilinged rooms divided by a central hallway: the master bedchamber, a sitting room, and a dining room and utility room that could be combined for special occasions. The four bedrooms upstairs would become the children's domain. There were porches covered with yellow jasmine and wisteria front and rear, called "piazzas," again in deference to the Charleston tradition.

Wyoming (c. 1811), birthplace of General States Rights Gist.
(Photograph by David Cisco)

Brick pathways led through formal gardens filled with roses, shrubs and gardenias. In the backyard stood the fireproof brick kitchen, smokehouse, and carriage house. Stables witnessed to the Gist family's love of horses. A large garden and orchard provided fruit and vegetables in season. There were fruit trees and gardens at the slave quarters too. Here two-and-three room cabins were home to the plantation's black work force and their families.[15]

The burgeoning slave population in the upcountry would have amazed the early pioneers. Eli Whitney's invention of the cotton gin made profitable large-scale production, and, as farmers became planters, black hands were needed to tend the fields through a long growing season. For Nathaniel Gist and the people of Union District, cotton was their only product and Columbia their only market. Boats carried the white cargo down the Broad River for sale in the Capital City.[16]

Even as he accumulated greater acreage and wealth, the master of Wyoming saw a dark cloud on the horizon, a threat to the prosperity of the exclusively agricultural region. In order to encourage a growing industrial base in the Northern States, the South and developing West were saddled with the expense of a protective tariff. For Gist and his neighbors, the rallying cry was "free trade!" Not that compromise was out of the question, but Southerners stood adamantly against both the ruinous tariff of 1828 and the revision being considered in 1831.

The South's champion and defender was another up-country South Carolina planter, Vice President of the United States John C. Calhoun. Building on principles set forth by Madison and Jefferson, Calhoun proposed a tactic already tested in the past by communities as diverse as Georgia and the New England States. Minority interests within the Union could be preserved by resorting to what Calhoun called nullification.

Nathaniel Gist and thousands of his countrymen were led irresistibly by the logic of Calhoun's argument: In ratifying the Constitution, South Carolina and the other states had freely entered a compact. Powers delegated by the states to the federal government were few and specific. Sovereignty had not been given up, nor shared, but was retained by the people of the several states. The United States of America were quite simply a league formed for their mutual benefit. Should the people of a state judge their rights or vital interests infringed upon, they could nullify the offending federal act. Such interposition of state authority would only void the enforcement of the specific law within the borders of the protesting state. If the dissenting state was overruled by three-fourths of the others, it could then submit to the decree of the majority, or voluntarily and peaceably leave the Confederation.

Proponents of states' rights were supremely confident in their position, charging that their adversaries were guilty of perverting the historical record to justify theories rejected

by the founding fathers. The facts presented were familiar
to Gist, for it was a history he had experienced himself. The
thirteen colonies emerged from the crucible of the Revolutionary War as distinct sovereignties, bound together in
"perpetual union" by the Articles of Confederation, but
jealous of their rights and prerogatives. When the federal
government proved inadequate, a new Constitution was ham-
mered out and presented to the states. The old Union that
the Articles proclaimed to be "perpetual" would be broken
up by the secession of individual states, free to ratify or re-
ject membership in a new league. No consolidated government was contemplated. Even Alexander Hamilton referred
to the states as "the parties to the contract," not the people
in the aggregate. "Every Constitution for the United States
must inevitably consist of a great variety of particulars,"
acknowledged Hamilton, "in which thirteen independent
States are to be accommodated in their interests or opinions
of interest."[17] That those independent states had no intention of abdicating their sovereignty was seen in the action
of several conventions that explicitly reserved their state's
right to secede even as they ratified the Constitution. "We
the people" of that document's preamble clearly referred to
the people organized as sovereign states.

The Union formed under the Constitution was, in Alexander Stephen's words, "a government instituted *by* States,
and *for* States, and all the functions it possesses, even in its
direct action on the individual citizens of the several States,
spring from and depend upon a Compact between the States
constituting it." The right of a member state to withdraw did
not signify that the system was weak, only that the people
were determined to avoid a "centralized despotic Empire."
The true strength of America's Federal Republic "lay in the
hearts of the people of the several States, and in no right
or power of keeping them together by coercion."[18]

Americans over the years tended toward a more na-
tionalistic interpretation of the federal government and its
role, and even most Southerners drew back from nullification, despite their abomination of the tariff. In the summer

of 1831 debate raged across the Palmetto State. Though unionists remained a respectable minority, proponents of nullification were gaining the upper hand in South Carolina. Calling themselves the "State Rights and Free Trade Party," nullifiers were in sometimes violent conflict with their fellow citizens, backers of President Andrew Jackson and national authority.[19]

Union District did not yet have its own newspaper, but disciples of Calhoun subscribed to the fiery *Mercury.* The Charleston daily published a three-times-a-week country edition that preached nullification to its wide rural readership. In late summer the paper reported formation of the "Union District Auxiliary State Rights and Free Trade Association." Later an unsigned letter declared, "I am proud to say that our Union District is to be found, gloriously contending on the side of Free Trade and State Rights."[20] Nathaniel Gist was chief among those local contenders. He read the *Mercury's* stirring call to action and shared the exhilaration of talking politics with like-minded neighbors.

By Saturday, September 3, 1831 the heat of a long summer began to moderate, but not the excitement on the Gist plantation. In the midst of the great constitutional controversy, Elizabeth Gist presented her husband with his seventh son and ninth child. She had also presented him with the opportunity to make a unique and unmistakable statement of his political faith. He named the little boy with blue eyes States Rights Gist.

As a boy, States Rights would learn how the crisis that inspired his name had postponed without resolving the issue of federal-versus-state supremacy. Congress indeed produced a tariff unacceptable to South Carolina, but even before it was to become law a state convention declared it "null and void." Congress countered with a force bill authorizing President Jackson to use the military of the United States against South Carolina. In this charged atmosphere a compromise was worked out by Henry Clay, replacing the tariff with a more palatable substitute. The state convention rescinded their original ordinance of nullification, but in a final gesture of defiance nullified the force bill. Both sides had backed down without losing face. Another generation would be call-ed upon to settle the question on the battlefield.

His family called him States. He remained the baby of the Gist household until the birth of James, last of the children, two years later. It is easy to imagine Sarah mother-ing her little brothers. Fifteen when States was born, she was the oldest of the children and the only girl; often in poor health, she was much like her mother in piety and strength of character. The boys were devoted to "Sister." She mar-ried her first cousin, John Gist, when States was six.

Joseph was twelve years older than States, followed by Nathaniel, Thomas, John, William and Robert. With so many brothers, States could count on plenty of help in learning to ride, shoot, and hunt in the forests and fields near home. The woods abounded with deer, wild turkeys, and raccoon. Robert even managed to capture a bear cub and raise it as a pet. Here was the kind of boyhood a city dweller would en-vy. Life was in tune with the seasons, with ample time for beloved outdoor adventures.[21]

Sunday was the Lord's Day. Each Sabbath found Elizabeth Gist and the children in the congregation of Fair Forest Presbyterian Church. "Mrs. Gist was a lady of great industry," remembered her pastor, "born in affluent cir-cumstances and always possessed of wealth, she might have excused herself from toil." Instead, she was devoted to the needs of her family, Wyoming Plantation and the larger com-munity. "She dried up the tears of orphans, poured balm in-to wounded hearts, directed and stimulated the efforts of children of the poor in laudable pursuits, gave encourage-ment to every good work and put a withering frown on vice."[22] To a male-dominated world preoccupied with horses, cotton, and politics, hers was compelling counterpoint.

States' pastor, Reverend James Hodge Saye, was also his teacher. Nathaniel Gist and neighbors John Wright and

John B. Glenn erected a small schoolhouse near Wyoming. Even before young Reverend Saye decided to relocate from McDonough, Georgia, he received specific instructions from Mr. Gist on how the little academy was expected to function: Classes must begin at 8 a.m. in the summer, 9 a.m. in winter; six weeks of vacation was more than adequate and tuition should not exceed $25. After making it clear who was in charge, the master of Wyoming suggested the preacher find a house and make necessary arrangements "if you conclude to come here as I hope you will." Curriculum included the basics of reading, spelling, writing, grammar, arithmetic, and geography. Young scholars were introduced to at least the fundamentals of Latin and Greek.[23]

Though denied college training himself, Nathaniel Gist was a firm believer in higher education. For States, the focus of anticipation was South Carolina College in Columbia. First there must be intensive preparation at a suitable fitting school; the kind of secondary education that would insure success in the classical curriculum of the antebellum college. Family tradition indicates Mount Zion Institute in the town of Winnsboro in Fairfield District as the academy chosen.[24] Not yet a teenager, States left the security of Wyoming for the first time to attend the school.

Chapter Two
"The World is the Battle Ground"

Winnsboro in the 1840's was a village of some five hundred souls, strongly Presbyterian, and best known as the home of Mount Zion. Incorporated as a "college" in 1785, the school never operated as an institution of higher learning. Instead it became one of South Carolina's illustrious nineteenth-century preparatory schools, attracting students from across the South. Its reputation was such that graduates were routinely accepted without examination by South Carolina College.

Boys often spent five years at Mount Zion, and States may have arrived there as early as age eleven. The school year began on January first and continued until the end of October, permitting the children a long Christmas holiday. The main building was an unimpressive structure, with small cabins on both sides for the fifty or sixty youngsters who boarded.

Mount Zion and Jacob W. Hudson were in the public mind synonymous. "Old J," as the boys nicknamed him, was the Institute's benevolent dictator and disciplinarian. Described as a handsome man and very strong, students stood in

awe of him. "He inflicted corporal punishment very sparing-
ly," recounted a former pupil, "and only upon the few most
incorrigible subjects. But it was enough to keep every boy
thinking what it would be if the thing were to happen to
himself." Sometimes he would exercise verbal wrath while
trimming a hickory, in the end to mercifully set it aside unus-
ed. Much misbehavior went unnoticed, especially fighting,
since Old J generally approved of the boys settling their
disputes with their fists. Though he never joined, Mr. Hudson attended and supported the local Presbyterian church.
His one vice was a well-known community secret: Paid very
well, he regularly lost it all at the poker table.

"Never did a teacher so impress the imagination of his
pupils," acknowledged former student Dr. William Porcher
DuBose. Latin was Hudson's strength and his speciality; the
only course he himself taught. On one visit to the North, Hudson hired Henri Harrise and Edward Maturin to teach French
and Greek respectively. Latin or Greek recitation preceded
breakfast at Mount Zion. Classes were in session ten hours
each day, the regimen abbreviated only slightly in winter.
Learning was intensive if not extensive. Natural science and
literature were ignored, but the few subjects taught were
thoroughly drilled into young minds.

Each fall, just before the beginning of the term at South
Carolina College, Mr. Hudson would concentrate his attention on the "college class." Satisfied he had done his best
by them, he would pen a letter of recommendation for each
scholar and send him on his way to Columbia. Armed with
such a missive, sixteen-year-old States arrived at the campus in early October 1847 and was admitted as a
sophomore.[1]

October was the perfect month for Columbia to display
her charm. The seemingly endless siege of another Carolina
summer had finally lifted. Her people were free again to savor
the cool, clear air; to relish the color and incense of autumn.
Hundreds of homes and businesses lined the unpaved
thoroughfares, the wooden capitol building (called the State

House) dominating from a prominence on Richardson (now Main) Street. Here States' older brother Joseph served in the State House of Representatives while cousin William Henry Gist represented Union in the Senate. Many city streets cut through virgin stands of pine, attesting to the fact that Columbia, as a planned community, remained as much vision as reality. Clustered behind a brick wall at the edge of town, but still within easy walking distance of the State House, stood the buildings of the South Carolina College.

The school was in its "golden age." Under the administration of President William Campbell Preston (1846-1851), generous state support permitted the erection of new buildings and the renovation of others on the tree-shaded campus drive called the Horseshoe. A magnificent library building housed 18,400 volumes at mid-century, more than Princeton or Columbia, and in the South equalled only by the University of Virginia. Students came from many states. Enrollment in 1849 reached 237, a total not surpassed until the twentieth century.[2]

South Carolina College, 1850.
(South Caroliniana Library)

A scholarly and prestigious faculty was primarily responsible for the college's stature. Most prominent was political
scientist Francis Lieber. Born in Berlin, and one of Blücher's
veterans of the Napoleonic Wars, the outspoken nationalist
was later forced to flee Prussia. After a stay in Boston editing
the *Encyclopedia Americana*, he took the professorship in
South Carolina as temporary employment. It was a position
he would hold for over two decades, time spent building a
reputation and writing his most important works. Ironically, Lieber established himself as America's great intellectual
exponent of nationalism while teaching in a college that was
becoming the seedbed of secession.[3]

A generation earlier, college President Thomas Cooper
had eloquently championed the rights of the states, his
staunch advocacy of decentralized government at the time
nearly as controversial as his religious deism. He once
created a sensation by boldly declaring that "we shall, before
long, be compelled to calculate the value of the union..."
Talk like that was disturbing in his day, but Cooper found
young men receptive to his views. Many former students of
his would in fact sign their names to the Ordinance of Secession in 1860.[4]

Faculty members Robert Henry, William Ellet, and Maximilian LaBorde, even without Lieber's national reputation,
still were genuine assets to the college. Most influential of
all was the brilliant and versatile James H. Thornwell.

As Presbyterian minister and denominational leader,
editor, orator, college professor and later college president,
Thornwell preached the fundamentalist faith that was in the
ascendancy in South Carolina. Thornwell's student addresses
rang with an evangelical urgency that even then drew sneers
from the lukewarm. Popular with the college boys, his sway
over them was considerable. In 1850 he summed up the
growing North-South controversy in terms States and his
fellow students could not misunderstand, an apocalyptic view
that left no room for compromise: "The parties in this conflict are not merely abolitionists and slaveholders — they are

atheists, socialists, communists, red republicans, jacobins on the one side, and the friends of order and regulated freedom on the other. In one word, the world is the battle ground — Christianity and atheism the combatants; and the progress of humanity the stake."[5]

It was a battle Southerners found thrust upon them. In the early years of the American republic slavery had existed in all thirteen states. Northern slaves were few, unimportant economically, and a gradual emancipation soon began. South of the Mason-Dixon line, many laborers were needed to grow cotton, tobacco, rice and sugar cane, and production of these staples spread together with the slave system. Yet even in the South the future of slavery was widely discussed and emancipation openly promoted. The British Empire had ended slavery without turmoil or bloodshed. John C. Calhoun, early in his career, saw slavery as a temporary institution, disappearing someday after outliving its usefulness.[6]

Then opinion began to harden. A New England coterie of zealots, eccentrics and liberal clergymen captured the emancipation movement. They concluded that to copy the successful British model of gradual, compensated freedom was to compromise with sin. In 1831, the year States was born, William Lloyd Garrison launched the *Liberator* in Boston with a fervent call for the immediate overthrow of slavery. That summer over fifty white men, women and children were slaughtered in Southampton County, Virginia in the Nat Turner slave revolt. The terror was quickly suppressed, but Southern open-mindedness was a casualty. "Garrison's uncanny genius to offend, insult, and lacerate in the name of a noble cause," wrote one historian, "gave the new [anti-slavery] society a birth defect it would never be able to remove."[7]

Southern churchmen were quick to cite the divine sanction of slavery throughout the Old and New Testaments. Slavery was as old as the human race, its defenders pointed out, and universally practiced except where proscribed by statute law. Washington and Jefferson had been slaveholders, and the Constitution itself recognized the institution, establishing a government that was to be a neutral agent of states having either system. To appeal to the "all men are created equal" phrase in the Declaration of Independence as an argument against slavery seemed to Southerners no more than sentimental sophistry. "Is it not palpably nearer the truth," asked Chancellor William Harper of South Carolina College, "to say that no man was ever born free, and that no two men were ever born equal?" Widespread Northern hypocrisy concerning blacks did not go unnoticed by Southern critics. Racism and a rigorous discrimination were openly practiced in those free states where abolitionists were loudest in "confessing the sins" of the slaveholding South. "Race prejudice seems stronger in those states that have abolished slavery than in those where it still exists," observed Alexis de Tocqueville in the mid 1830's, "and nowhere is it more intolerant than in those states where slavery was never known."[8]

At South Carolina College no ground would be conceded to the enemy, though combat for the moment remained verbal. Rhetoric was a weapon well-chosen; skill with the spoken word much admired and sought-after in Southern society. On the Columbia campus students honed their oratory and tried out their arguments in the Clariosophic and Euphradian societies. All students joined one debating club or the other. States would cast his lot with the Clariosophics.

John C. Calhoun and Andrew Jackson, among others, had in the past accepted honorary society membership. In 1849 the admiring young Clariosophics voted to extend the honor to professor Louis Agassiz of Harvard. Questions philosophical or religious might on occasion claim their attention, but debate inevitably returned to politics. "The circumstances under which South Carolina might leave the Union" was considered a lively topic, but not the constitutional legality of such action. Students reflected the consensus that had developed in the state: The wisdom of secession was a subject over which gentlemen might differ — the right of the state to take the step was a settled question. For the son of Nathaniel Gist this was a doctrine unchallenged since childhood, in maturity unassailable.[9]

Records do not show where States lived his first year at college. Possibly he stayed in town, as dormitory space was overtaxed. In his junior and senior years he roomed with a studious young man from Beaufort, South Carolina named Thomas E. Screven. He and Tom first shared a room in DeSaussure and then Rutledge, the two oldest buildings on campus.[10] They took their meals at Steward's Hall, as did all the students, and marched together to compulsory morning chapel services. High-spirited and intensely proud, inordinate numbers of his peers continually faced suspension for their pranks and protests. To States the discipline was not burdensome, steeled as he was by the years at Mount Zion.

Mr. Hudson's insistence on a thorough grounding in the classics was paying off too. States was not dismayed having to study Tacitus, Livy and Latin composition his first year. Included also in the sophomore curriculum was plane and spherical trigonometry; geometry; conic sections; history of the Middle Ages; logic and rhetoric; and elocution. Latin composition again faced the junior class, as did the writings of Cicero, Horace, Juvenal and Persius. There were classes in differential and integral calculus; chemistry and magnetism; modern history; criticism and elocution; moral philosophy; political philosophy; and physiology. A course called sacred literature and evidences of Christianity rounded out the year. Seniors tackled Latin and Greek composition. Astronomy; civil engineering; political economy; political ethics; philosophy of the mind; geology; mineralogy and agricultural chemistry were new subjects introduced to scholars their final year.[11]

States and congenial roommate Tom could congratulate themselves. Three years of diligence earned for both of them graduation with honors. Classes ended in July, but they were required to return in December, the traditional month for graduation, to receive their Latin-inscribed diplomas.

In spite of weather so inclement that students were excused from attending, the House and Senate formed in procession, somehow making their way to a college chapel "crowded to excess." Those graduating with honors were privileged to deliver a short address to the assembled multitude. States chose as his topic "Party Spirit." Though we have no record of its content, "There was no speech made that was not creditable to a young speaker in both style and elocution," reported the Columbia *Telegraph.* "Many of the subjects were calculated to task the maturest powers of thought and all the speeches gave evidence not only of ability and talent, but industry, which is still greater than talent."[12]

Party spirit was indeed rife in South Carolina at midcentury. Back in the summer of 1846, an obscure Pennsylvania congressman named David Wilmot had proposed the prohibition of slavery from all territory acquired in the Mexican War. That blatant challenge to Southern equality in the Union set off a storm of protest in South Carolina, over the next few years moving the state increasingly toward secession. While many hesitated for fear that South Carolina would be isolated if she acted alone, the Gist family came to be identified with those demanding immediate state action. Young States demonstrated unusual maturity in recognizing the perils of factionalism. If South Carolina was to precipitate a revolution she must herself be united.

The state would enter the new decade not only divided but leaderless. On March 31, 1850 word flashed down the telegraph wire from Washington that Calhoun was dead. His consuming passion had been to find permanent security for his beloved South within the Union, but confidence had eluded him. Outvoted in Congress, the agrarian South eventually would find herself at the mercy of the dominant section if she stayed in the Union. Yet prospects for the success of a Southern bid for independence also grew steadily dimmer as the years passed and the North waxed stronger.

South Carolina secessionists proclaimed that compromise would only postpone the life-and-death struggle. Because the Palmetto State was so far in advance of opinion elsewhere in the South, sister states shunned her leadership. When a convention of Southerners met in Nashville in June 1850 delegates could only agree to a demand for equality for the region. In late summer the United States Congress, after much debate, passed the Compromise Measures of 1850. California was admitted as a free state, the slave trade was abolished in the District of Columbia, and territories gained from Mexico were opened to settlers of all persuasions. The North's major concession was the Fugitive Slave Law, providing for the effective return of runaways.

Optimists North and South hoped the slavery controversy was settled at last, and South Carolina secessionists found themselves increasingly isolated. In May 1851 a call for immediate secession by the Charleston convention of the Southern Rights Association created an unexpected backlash. Greenville's Benjamin F. Perry founded the *Southern Patriot* to openly promote unionism in the Palmetto State. Secessionist sentiment still predominated in the South Carolina lowcountry and the upcountry districts of Laurens, Fairfield and Union. But for the most part moderates held sway. South Carolina would, for the time being, take no unilateral action.[13]

Through the months of political uncertainty States proceeded as best he could with his career plans. The son of a wealthy, influential and socially prominent family, States would enjoy every advantage available to the planter class. But privilege demanded responsibility in Nathaniel Gist's view. A gentleman must prepare himself for leadership and service. The father expected much from his son and had never been disappointed. Whatever calling States would follow, a college education was a commendable beginning, a foundation that many leading men of the older generation did not possess. But the most important preparation, virtually a prerequisite for success, was a background in the law.

Though practicing attorneys were relatively few, legions of respectable and responsible men in public as well as private life began as lawyers. Joseph F. Gist had been admitted to the bar a decade earlier, his practice of law leading to state political office. As there was no law school in the state, legal training was a task he and most others began on their own. An aspiring young man most often would study under the guidance of an established lawyer, availing himself of his benefactor's knowledge, experience, and library.

Unionville was home to six attorneys in 1850, and to one or more of these men States likely turned for help. Burdened with books he would make his way between Unionville and Wyoming.[14] Home may have at first seemed the ideal place for reading the law, but his dissatisfaction would only increase as self-study's limitations became apparent. States was in the habit of excelling, not merely getting by. He wanted a legal education second to none, and if such training was unavailable within the state he could not be faulted for looking elsewhere. With the secession crisis over, he was free to venture forth in search of the finest institution in America. That reputation, friends and former teachers could not deny, belonged to the Law School of Harvard University.

Many of the region's brightest young men had sought a "Yankee" education — to return surprisingly untainted by the exposure, indeed more devoted than ever to Southern values. Harvard Law School's course of study consisted of three terms of six months each, after which was granted the degree of Bachelor of Laws. No entrance examination was required, State's college degree was sufficient for admission.[15]

His mind was made up. He was accepted, and in the fall of 1851 set out for Boston. The journey itself was surely an education and an adventure for the twenty-year-old. Stage lines connected Unionville to Charleston where passage could be booked for the voyage up the coast. As his ship slipped anchor and moved with the tide down the Cooper River there was a salty tang in the breeze. From the rail he could see the rooftops and steeples of the city receding behind the seawall-promenade they called the battery. Off the starboard bow loomed half-finished, yet already grim-visaged, Fort Sumter.

Harvard Law School as it appeared during young Gist's student days. *(Courtesy of the Harvard University Archives)*

Finally arriving in the Massachusetts capital, the boy from the red hills of the Carolina upcountry must have stared wide-eyed at the magnificent and historic old city. Already a metropolis of 140,000, Boston well-represented the North's expanding wealth, population and power. Horse-drawn omnibuses transported passengers through the crowded dockside slums, past the business district and fashionable Beacon Hill, on across the Charles River to Cambridge and the University.

Harvard's Law School was established in 1817 and for nineteen years had been quartered in the Ionic-columned temple some thought the most beautiful on campus. Students were gathering from across the country, drawn by a growing national renown. The ninety-four young men who enrolled in States' first term would increase to over one-hundred the next year.[16]

Boston was the very capital of the abolition movement — a gathering place where true believers could thunder damnation to their countrymen to the South. Here Garrison had publicly burned the American Constitution, denouncing it as "a covenant with Death and an agreement with Hell." Yet young Southerners at Harvard were to a remarkable extent welcomed by conservative Cambridge families, a society that abolitionist Senator Charles Sumner dismissed as "bigoted, narrow, provincial and selfish..."[17] Sumner's venomous hatred for the South was well-known. Two years previous to States' arrival the Senator had been made to endure the wrath of Harvard Law School's Southern boys, interrupted by their shouts and hisses as he delivered a free-soil speech in Cambridge. In May of 1851 Ralph Waldo Emerson castigated the new compromise, speaking at Cambridge City Hall, and received the same reception.[18] The university was, by and large, an island of pragmatism in a seething sea of irrationality. "Curiously enough," wrote historian Samuel Eliot Morrison, "the students of that day had a better means of estimating the situation than the Massachusetts public; for there was a large delegation of Southern students both in college and Law School, most of them members of leading political families, who left no doubt in their classmates' minds that the alternative to compromise was immediate secession..."[19] The Southern presence at Harvard is perhaps one of the least-known facets of the great university's pre-war history. No fewer than 257 Harvard men would fight in the Confederate army, the Law School alone educating three future generals in gray.[20]

Theophilus Parsons, Dane Professor of Law; and Joel
Parker, Royall Professor, each had a distinct teaching style.
Parker made his assignments from the text and covered the
material to the letter; Parsons emphasized discussion and
questioning. According to school regulations, students "are
[at] liberty to elect what studies they will pursue according
to their own view of their wants and attainments." Offered
were courses in real property, equity, constitutional law,
pleading, bills and notes, domestic relations, evidence, ship-
ping and admiralty, bailments, wills and administration, part-
nership, insurance and arbitration.[21]

Gone were the compulsory appurtenances, the discipline
that States had by now come to associate with schooling.
Parker and Parsons provided an academic environment that,
if anything, provoked criticism for being too loosely struc-
tured. "There were no examinations," remembered former
student Joseph H. Choate, "attendance at the lectures was
voluntary, but most of the students were very zealous in their
attendance. There was no cramming...Whoever wanted to
learn, learned quite enough."[22] Young scholars coming to
lecture unprepared sat in a predesignated corner of the hall,
there exempt from professorial questioning. This sanctuary
the students dubbed "Oregon," its settlers seemingly isolated
from the world of learning.

The pride and heart of the Law School was its interna-
tionally-renowned library of 12,000 volumes, thought to be
the largest collection of law books in the English language.
Assisting in the library was a fellow student of States named Christopher Columbus Langdell, the man who would one
day make a sweeping reorganization of the study of law at
Harvard.[23]

In a few years States would read in the newspaper of a
Boston mob, passions stirred by an abolitionist rally at
Faneuil Hall, attempting to storm the courthouse to free a
runaway slave.[24] This was in the future; the months of States'
residence proved relatively calm. He must have been
dismayed though, at the credulity of the Northern public as

they devoured an inflammatory novel called *Uncle Tom's Cabin.* Published in Boston while States was at Harvard, Harriet Beecher Stowe's best-seller fanned the fires of abolitionism.

That summer States was visited by an old friend. Professor Thornwell, now President of South Carolina College, came in search of methods for bettering his own institution and was graciously received by Harvard's President Jared Sparks. As a youth Thornwell had studied for a time at Harvard, but left tormented by the frigid weather and what he perceived as the school's unitarian heresies. Most of what Thornwell experienced on this trip to Cambridge met with his approbation, but the irreligion of the place still darkened his view. "Though I have received nothing but kindness and courtesy in Boston and Cambridge," wrote Thornwell to his wife, "I sigh for home."[25]

Perhaps the visit of Dr. Thornwell reminded States just how much he too missed home. About this time he discovered that old poem "Gertrude of Wyoming," and was affected by it as his father had been. He wrote to sister-in-law Mary (brother Nathaniel's wife), then at Wyoming plantation awaiting the birth of her second child. If a girl, States pleaded, give her the name Gertrude. The child was indeed a girl, and Mary went along with the romantic whim of the homesick expatriot.[26]

Facing another Northern winter, yet one term short of the required stay, this South Carolinian was anxious to go home. On October 1, 1852 Professor Parker signed a certificate verifying States' attendance of one year and commending the young man for having been "diligent in his studies and exemplary in his conduct and demeanor."[27] Though there would be no LLB degree,[28] States had what he had come for, and a great deal more. To his graduation with honors from South Carolina College was added the prestige of a Harvard Law School education, certainly remarkable preparation for any small-town lawyer. Equally valuable was exposure to another culture. For one year he had opportunity first-hand to weigh arguments he had never before heard and observe sectional prejudices other than his own. States returned to the Palmetto State a wiser young man, lighthearted to be coming home and anxious to get on with his career.

"I do accordingly recommend him to the Profession," read Judge Parker's certificate, "as entitled to their respect and confidence." But no recommendation, however, could make him a lawyer. Young Mr. Gist must first pass the state examination, and that required further study in South Carolina law. This time he hit the books with a new confidence and professional familiarity, and by spring felt ready to go before the examiner. Traditionally these inquiries were quite informal, the judge already acquainted with the applicant and his qualifications. On May 10, 1853, States Rights Gist appeared in the Court of Appeals in Columbia and was found to be "duly qualified to act as an attorney in the courts of law." Proudly the new lawyer took an oath of allegiance to the state of South Carolina, another oath required of the profession, and headed back to the little courthouse town of Unionville to set up practice.[29]

Soon an advertisement appeared in the *Unionville Journal:*

Law Notice
Arthur & Gist
Attorneys at Law
Will practice in the courts of the Northern
Circuit, Offices at Unionville, S.C.
B.F. Arthur   S.R. Gist[30]

Gist outfitted his new office with an impressive mahogany desk, chairs, and bookcase. A basic set of forty-five law books were added to his eclectic accumulation of other volumes. Fortuitously, he found for himself an experienced partner. Benjamin Franklin Arthur was five years Gist's senior, having practiced law with a brother in Columbia before moving to Unionville in 1851. A small, frail man, he was well-liked and readily accepted by his new neighbors. He rose to prominence in the Masonic lodge and served as Judge Advocate in a local militia regiment.

Gist quickly discovered what Arthur already knew: The hard work of a circuit-riding lawyer was usually routine if not downright dull. He began, as all did, a criminal lawyer in General Sessions Court. Each term saw Gist and his colleagues arguing petty cases before jurors influenced less by reason and judicial subleties than emotional oratory. Nevertheless, lasting friendships were formed and his name began to be known in the Districts of Spartanburg, York and Chester.[31] He was paying the price required of all newcomers to the profession. Greater challenges would come soon enough.

Chapter Three
"Nodding Plumes and Brilliant Uniforms"

Captain States Rights Gist. The title seemed to fit, and he looked so handsome in his dark-blue uniform, set off with two rows of brass buttons. Splendid silver epaulets, white gloves, red sash and a white plumed hat completed the picture. The new commanding officer of the Johnson Rifles proudly took the salute of his sixty officers and men, his company named for the governor who provided their weaponry. It was attached to the 35th Regiment, 9th Brigade, 5th Division, South Carolina Militia.

Gist was elected commander of the Rifles shortly after his return to Unionville. Brother Joseph was adjutant general of the 5th Division with the rank of colonel, and law partner Benjamin Arthur was a first lieutenant on the staff of the 35th Regiment.[1] Militia leadership was natural for a promising lawyer; for a gentleman of Gist's family background, education and position, almost expected.

Military training provided a welcome break from routine and an outlet for the high-spirited and ambitious young man. But there were also more serious considerations. Facing a future increasingly uncertain, the Palmetto State began looking to its long-neglected militia for reassurance, and Gist, as a public-spirited South Carolinian, certainly felt a responsibility to become involved. He began to fear that sectional strife would eventually result from what he called the "fungus growth" of abolitionism's new Republican Party. Thomas N. Dawkins, a neighbor and friend since Gist's boyhood, credited the young Captain's motivation to well-thought-out political goals: "He was educated and a firm believer in the reserved rights of the States, a strict constructionist...determined to render what aid he could in defense of his principles if the necessity arose. He advocated secession and was ready to sustain it..."[2]

Under the Militia Laws of 1841, the state was geographically apportioned into five divisions. Each consisted of two infantry brigades, they in turn made up of regiments and companies and supported by cavalry and artillery. Socially-elite volunteer companies, such as the Johnson Rifles, were incorporated into the system. The governor was commander-in-chief, assisted by a full-time adjutant and inspector general elected by the legislature. With certain exemptions, all white males from eighteen to forty-five were subject to duty in the form of quarterly drills and annual reviews. Commissioned officers of the brigade elected their brigadier general, and division officers a major general; the victor then appointing his staff officers. At the company and regimental levels officers were chosen by vote of the men in the ranks. Discipline and attention to duty at all levels were shored up by an elaborate array of fines.[3]

"The present condition of the militia system is becoming a subject of great importance," acknowledged the *Unionville Journal* in the summer of 1854. "There can be no doubt," the editor added with charitable understatement, "that the present system is attended with many evils and inconveniences..."[4]

Harsher critics saw the militia for what it undeniably was — a fighting force virtually useless. Men of prominence in the cities and towns preferred volunteer companies. Clad in impressive if impractical uniforms, they usually took on the character of social clubs with a military flavor. Many country units went through the motions of drilling with sticks for muskets and no uniforms at all. Because of the drunkenness that inevitably accompanied "training," the militia was condemned as a poor influence on youthful recruits.[5]

Though the tramping warriors seldom knew their right from their left, parades and reviews were popular. Such shows seemed to be the militia's sole reason for being. These spectacles "occasioned a lively turnout of the people," one participant remembered, "both ladies and gentlemen, not connected with the troops, to witness the display of officer's uniforms, and bright caparisoned steeds, the stately tread of the 'muster men,' listen to the rattle of the drums and inspiring strains of the fifes, and horns of the rural bands."[6]

In addition to "repelling invasion," the militia was charged with responsibility for internal security. Companies were divided into squads for the purpose of patrolling. At nights and on Sundays these amateurish policemen would walk their beat, supposedly to prevent illegal assemblies of blacks and insure that individual slaves had their master's permission to be out. One realist remembered that "this system had dwindled down to a farce, and was only engaged in by some of the youngsters, more in a spirit of fun and frolic than to keep order in the neighborhood."[7]

The *Yorkville Enquirer* recommended that young men could perhaps be trained in the state's military schools and rapidly promoted to high rank in the militia, thereby forcing "important and radical changes." This desperate call for action came after the editor attended a regimental review in August 1855, a pleasant social event presided over by Brigadier General Oliver Evans Edwards. Once again those concerned with military preparedness were reminded that the 9th Brigade exhibited the same glaring defects that crippled South Carolina's entire militia system. Groping for words to adequately express his frustration, the newspaper-

man condemned what he saw as a "disordered, deranged —
we had almost said useless organization."[8]

Through the decade of the 1850's came repeated calls
for reform. Finally by 1858 the General Assembly would
authorize a commission to study militia problems and come
up with a plan for reorganization. The majority report in 1859
called for an end to abuses (such as officers appointing the
grossly unqualified), and for more emphasis on training.
Their proposals aimed at a smaller, yet higher quality, force.[9]
Other reports varied in the particulars, though almost any
change would have been worth a try. Still, nothing was done.
Genuinely concerned officers would continue to perform their
duties in a system bent on handicapping efficiency.

As the regulations stipulated, Captain Gist called his
company together about every three months for a day of instruction, meeting typically at the Union Courthouse on a
Saturday.[10] What he and they actually learned of soldiering
from these encounters was skimpy indeed. Even the best led
and motivated units had little time for serious training
beyond the rudiments of drill and ceremonies and perhaps
a little target practice. Yet Captain Gist applied himself to
the study of tactics, a diligence that raised eyebrows.[11]

If militia service provided him with no more than an introduction to military science, there were still fundamental
lessons to be learned. In a military that elected its own officers, leadership (where it existed at all) involved more than
the ability to bark orders and stand on one's authority. If a
popularity contest represented one form of failure,
authoritarianism was another. These individualistic South
Carolinians had to be motivated, not pushed. Firmness was
respected only when gloved with tact and persuasion. The
Johnson Rifles was a school in the art of management, a confidence course in their commander's ability to handle men.
The gift of leadership he discovered in himself and developed
on the training grounds of Unionville would prove invaluable.

Other militia officers were becoming acquainted with the Captain, and his law practice insured that the name States R. Gist would become increasingly recognized in the South Carolina upcountry. Positive and cheerful, he exhibited a generosity and charm that endeared him to his neighbors. Gist was "a young man of decided promise," according to one who knew him, "possessing intellect of a high order, well cultivated, agreeable manners with firmness and decision of character..." If there was whispered resentment of his family's wealth and political connections, his winning ways and genuine ability could only disarm critics.[12]

In December of 1854, James Hopkins Adams, wealthy planter and politician from Richland District, was elected governor. Adams was an old family friend, and on December 18, one of his first acts as commander-in-chief of the militia was to appoint Captain Gist his aide-de-camp with the rank of lieutenant colonel.[13] Under the militia laws of South Carolina, the governor was authorized to commission ten such officers. Formal duties were nil and he was not required to relinquish command of the Rifles. Nevertheless, the recognition must have been gratifying. The elite of antebellum South Carolina were hearing of the accomplishments of this young man from Union who took the militia seriously. No crusader, he retained a common-sense realism, yet he had a vision and desire for reform.

In early January 1856 his opportunity came. Oliver E. Edwards resigned as commanding officer of the 9th Brigade and Major General James H. Williams set April 26 as election day to choose a replacement. Quickly a paid notice appeared in the newspapers: "We are authorized to announce Col. S.R. Gist of Union, as candidate for BRIGADIER GENERAL of the Ninth Brigade, S.C.M." Voting from eleven until three on the designated Saturday, the officers of the brigade along with local officers of the division staff ratified the unopposed candidate. States Rights Gist, at age twenty-four, was a brigadier general.[14]

Changes began to be noticed in the regiments of the brigade, improvements that the newspapers reported without venturing to assign credit. "We saw no brawling, no rowdyism, no drunkenness," heralded the Spartanburg *Carolina Spartan* in describing a June training session. "We hope to see all muster fields as free from such scenes."[15]

Glenn Springs in Spartanburg District was a militia mustering point as well as a popular vacation site, and here in August 1856 Governor Adams brought his family while he made the rounds of upstate reviews. On the twelfth, General Gist hosted a ball in the Governor's honor at Spartanburg's Palmetto House Hotel. An observer noted the presence of "several bright stars of the gender feminine."[16] One of them could have been the Governor's daughter Jane Margaret Adams. Now fifteen, Janie probably remembered States from childhood. And it was perhaps about this time that he began to take notice of the young woman who would one day become his wife.

For the General's first full-scale review the August weather was uncommonly mild. "Adjutant and Inspector General R.G.M. Dunovant, General Williams and General S.R. Gist, accompanied by their respective staffs were in attendance," noted the *Yorkville Enquirer,* "and with their 'nodding plumes' and brilliant uniforms presented quite a martial appearance."

The reporter declared that the "citizen soldiery" must somehow be convinced that militia service was a no-nonsense exercise of patriotic duty. "It is almost entire want of this spirit that has brought the system into such disrepute. Nothing but a genuine military spirit and zeal on the part of the officers can ever restore it to favor." At the close of the ceremonies Gist complimented the men on their performance. He made a "short but spirited" speech stressing the need for readiness, implying that neither uncritical praise nor blanket condemnation was appropriate. "General Gist," in the words of the *Enquirer* "defended the Militia system from the cheers and jeers of the careless and indifferent..."[17]

If the system could be saved by a revival of "military spirit and zeal," the new commanding general was determined that his brigade pioneer the movement. Where a cavalry review might formerly be occasion for pageantry and self-congratulation, now there was "searching scrutiny and conferences with the Colonel on the deficiency in dress and equipment." General Gist insisted his citizen-soldiers be well-drilled and saw to it they were well-armed. To encourage competitive excellence he presented a silver and gold goblet to the Morgan Rifles as an annual prize for their best marksman. Emphasis on the martial virtues inevitably enhanced pride and morale. Within a year the regiments of the 9th Brigade were receiving handsome compliments on their performance and readiness. Witnessing an encampment in July 1857, one local reporter commented that in facing hardships, the conduct of the men was a "stern rebuke" to cynical detractors.[18]

Editor Samuel W. Melton of the *Yorkville Enquirer* was himself a militia officer and for this reason apologized to his readers for being so complimentary of General Gist. "We must nevertheless speak out the opinion, expressed by all, that the Brigade has been peculiarly fortunate in the choice of a commander... Our military wish the General a prosperous career; and when the occasion offers, will cordially aid in his advancement to a still higher position."[19]

For Gist's twenty-sixth birthday, the proprietor of the Palmetto House Hotel gave a ball in honor of the popular young General, the party "graced by many fair ladies and brave men in brilliant and flashing uniforms." According to the reporter, "The General himself seemed to enjoy the occasion hugely, and chased the merry hours with flying feet, with no rude alarms of war to disturb the fascinating amusement..."[20]

High compliments became common, Gist's command declared by Governor Robert Francis Withers Alston equal to the best in the state. "We have never seen a more lively spirit manifested, or a more earnest endeavor on the part of those entrusted with command..." applauded the editor of the *Enquirer* in late summer 1859. The General attended to his duties with customary efficiency, "his manner and high-toned bearing and thorough accomplishments as an officer winning the golden opinions of both rank and file."[21] None realized they had witnessed Gist's final review as 9th Brigade commander.

Chapter Four
"No Flag But the Palmetto"

Few families were more deeply involved than the Gists in the political life of antebellum South Carolina. States Rights Gist's uncle, United States Congressman Joseph Gist, began the tradition. Brother Joseph was a longtime member of the State House and Senate. Most illustrious was the career of William Henry Gist.

William was born in Charleston in 1807 the son of Francis Gist, Nathaniel's brother and business partner. Little is known of William's mother except that she was unmarried and gave up custody of the child to his father. Uncle Nathaniel became guardian for a time after Francis' death. The stigma of an illegitimate birth was no handicap to the ambitious young man. William studied at Thomas Cooper's South Carolina College, though he was expelled in a student rebellion and never graduated.

In early manhood young William Henry Gist had to stand trial for murder. Supposedly the incident was an affair of honor "over some remarks about a lady," and he was acquitted. Later in life active membership in the Methodist Church and devotion to the temperance movement burnished a reputation for piety. He became a wealthy planter, established with his family at "Rose Hill," their Tyger River home. In 1840

William Henry Gist, South Carolina's "Secession Governor."
(Rose Hill Plantation State Park. Photograph by David Cisco)

Rose Hill Plantation State Park, Union County, South Carolina.
Home of Governor William Henry Gist.
(Photograph by David Cisco)

voters first sent him to the State House of Representatives and after 1844 he represented Union District in the South Carolina Senate. Fellow legislators elected him lieutenant governor in 1848, and in 1858 to the two-year term of governor. A consistent adherent to the militant states' rights position, he would play a leading part in the drama about to begin.[1]

Palmetto State secessionists in 1851 and 1852 had hoped the state would take the lead in moving for independence, only to find other Southerners unwilling to follow and South Carolina itself divided. The people were exhausted and wanted a respite from factionalism after years of political agitation. General prosperity and at least lukewarm acceptance of the 1850 Compromise encouraged a period of relative contentment in 1853 and 1854.

Complacency, however, was short-lived. Although protectionism persisted, the growth of abolitionism was far more sinister. The sectional struggle over slavery in the territories continued, in Kansas leading to open warfare. Some Northern states were even defiantly interfering with the lawful return of runaways.

A majority of South Carolinians as yet held back from Governor Gist's secessionism, though there was unanimity on the basic issues. Conservatives advocated Southern support of the Democratic Party, arguing it had proven a reliable ally. Election of President James Buchanan in 1856 bolstered optimisim and strengthened their position. Secessionists on the other hand were frankly distrustful of any alliance that included non-Southerners, convinced that safety and prosperity could only be found in a Southern confederacy free from anti-slavery zealots.

Abolitionists continually inflamed Southern fears. John Brown, obsessed for decades with combatting slavery, began a violent crusade for the liberation of the slaves. In May 1856, he and his sons and followers murdered five Kansas settlers suspected of Southern opinions. Avoiding arrest, he planned to lead a slave insurrection in the South.

Financed by Northern abolitionists, Brown in October 1859 led his sons and a band of followers to Harper's Ferry, Virginia. There, he captured the Federal Arsenal, but United States Marines under the command of Colonel Robert E. Lee soon captured Brown and his followers. He was brought to trial and hung after being found guilty of treason and murder.

The North's reaction to Brown's execution, many hailing him as a martyr, shocked South Carolina.[2] Already under psychological and economic pressure, an atmosphere of uneasiness dominated the state as vigilance committees organized and militia patrol duty took on a new urgency. The conservative majority, their illusions challenged by widespread Northern fanaticism, began seriously to question expectations for continued liberty and security within the

Union. Yet to the disgust of fire-eaters (as immediate secessionists were called), conservatives met in early April 1860 to again choose delegates to the Democratic convention. The national party would be meeting later that month, in Charleston of all places. Those South Carolinians who held back from disunion hoped against hope that once again the South could control the party, defeat what they called the "Black Republicans" and somehow keep the country together.

Elizabeth Gist had for several years suffered a decline in health. Her death in June 1859 was a time of sorrow, not only for her family but also for a wide circle of friends. Grief over the loss of his mother came as the General struggled with a decision about his future in the militia.

After more than three years as brigade commander, Gist may have felt the goals he set for himself were largely accomplished. Hints of his resignation brought protests from friends. The *Yorkville Enquirer* maintained that "it is a public loss to be deprived of the services of such an officer." The editor praised Gist's uncommon military abilities and added that he combined professional accomplishments with "the tone and bearing of that most enviable character — the well bred gentleman... We trust that a sober second thought will persuade the General to extend the office..."[3] John Brown's raid coming only a few weeks later proved sobering indeed. With the state shocked and fearful, it was no time to resign a militia commission.

Soon after taking office, Governor Gist had honored his cousin with appointment as the Commander-in-Chief's "Especial Aid-de-Camp." It was another indication that General Gist had found a place in the Governor's inner circle. In a September 1859 letter to advisor and confidant Beaufort T. Watts, Governor Gist told of plans to rent a furnished house in the Capital City during the upcoming legislative session. Besides Watts, invited to share the bachelor quarters were legislators James Simons and Henry

Buist, and States Rights Gist. "We intend to get a Charleston Cook & Butler & get supplies of all we need direct from the city," wrote the chief executive. "Won't we have a fine time." But there was no escaping the loneliness of leadership. During the final year of his administration the Governor would find the responsibilities almost overwhelming. On May 6, 1860 Governor Gist complained of exhaustion and admitted the recent political turmoil "has entirely unnerved me & I am down below zero."[4]

It would be natural for the Governor to turn to his cousin for friendship and support. And perhaps it was the Governor's plight that finally forced General Gist to make a decision. In early April, after nearly four years of outstanding service, States Rights Gist resigned his commission as commanding general of the 9th Brigade.[5]

In April a desperately divided Democratic national convention met in Charleston. Southerners demanded a platform committed to congressional protection of slavery in the territories, while Northern delegates feared the political repercussions in their home states of such a plank. Defeated on the floor of the convention, the Southern delegates walked out. Later the two factions separately reconvened to nominate rival presidential contenders: Senator Stephen A. Douglas of Illinois by the Northern wing, and Vice President John C. Breckinridge of Kentucky, champion of the South. Abraham Lincoln would face a divided opposition. As the campaign entered the summer of 1860, it became increasingly likely that the abolitionist "Black Republicans" would emerge victorious. A strictly sectional party, representing a minority of the electorate, was poised to elect Abraham Lincoln to the power of the White House.

South Carolinians had been considering the possibility of a Republican triumph for some time, fire-eaters counting on a Lincoln victory to make real their dream of a Southern confederacy. Now from across the state a consensus began to coalesce, a growing determination that the Palmetto State could never be part of a republic ruled by abolitionists. A tiny handful clung stubbornly to unionism, but by summer the overwhelming majority found the conclusion inescapable: The state's response to a Lincoln triumph must be secession.

The debate now took a new turn as disagreement developed over what course secession should take. "Separate state actionists" were convinced that South Carolina's secession would be followed inevitably by other like-minded states. In any event, they argued, she should act fearlessly and go out alone. "Cooperationists" argued that it would be safer and more feasible for three or more states to secede together. On this point alone was there contention as election day approached.

With secession fever mounting in South Carolina, Governor Gist determined to test sentiment elsewhere. Evidence that neighboring states might indeed follow South Carolina in leaving the Union would greatly strengthen the argument for separate state action. And if Southern cooperation was called for then someone must take the initiative. Either way, the time had come for frank communication between the Southern governors.

Interstate diplomacy of such consequence required careful preparation and handling. Secrecy was essential. If the newspapers learned of the exchange of views its purpose would be defeated, candid expression dissolving into denial and misunderstanding. With the election only weeks away, time was also a factor. Correspondence through the mails would be slow and impersonal. Telegraphic communication was instant yet insecure. For this extraordinary mission the Governor needed a special courier, an agent capable of meeting with the chief executives and conveying facts and impressions home again. A family member, well-educated and eloquent, States Rights Gist seemed the ideal personal emissary. The fact that he still held the title "general" lent authority; his name itself was almost providential.

From his Unionville residence on October fifth, the Governor wrote identical letters to the chief executives of North Carolina, Georgia, Florida, Alabama, Mississippi and Louisiana.[6] North Carolina was probably included in this roster of Deep South or Cotton States due more to proximity than fraternity. Texas, ripe for secession overtures, may have seemed for the moment too distant — or simply unrepresented by stubborn unionist Governor Sam Houston.

Governor Gist in his letter predicted the election of Abraham Lincoln and stated plainly that South Carolina would call a secession convention in response. His opinion was that the state would only leave the Union if another went out first, or if others were sure to follow. He urged other states, if they were to call conventions, to meet the same day. Gist assured his fellow governors that their replies would be confidential, promising that he would share their views only with "reliable and leading men in consultation for the safety of our State and the South..." The mission was veiled in such secrecy that even secretary and advisor Watts was not consulted.[7]

Over the next four weeks by railroad and stage line, States Rights Gist made a circuitous tour of Dixie. North Carolina's John W. Ellis was first to receive the letter, on October 12. Though Ellis described himself as a "States-Rights man, believing in the sovereignty and reserved powers of the States," his reply to Governor Gist contained little to encourage secessionists in South Carolina. In his opinion the election of Lincoln would not in itself be grounds for dissolution of the Union. But neither would North Carolina be party to "the monstrous doctrine of coercion" of states that chose independence.

Joseph E. Brown of Georgia acknowledged receipt of Governor Gist's letter "by the hand of General Gist, with whom I have had a free interchange of opinions." Brown gave the General an advance copy of his soon-to-be-delivered message to the legislature and predicted that while Georgia would not secede alone, "The action of other States may greatly influence the action of the people of this State." Alabama too, according to her Governor Andrew Barry Moore, would not secede first, but would cooperate with two or more others in going out. Mississippi's Governor John J. Pettus expected Southern unity in the face of the Republican threat, "yet I do not believe Mississippi can move alone." If another state seceded first however, "I think Mississippi will go with her." Louisiana's chief executive Thomas O. Moore, writing from Alexandria, made a long and discouraging reply. Louisiana, according to Governor Moore, was unprepared and unwilling to leave the Union. He suggested a convention of Southern States to decide what to do if Lincoln came to power, implying at least that Louisiana would go along with the majority.

Florida's Governor was apparently absent from Tallahassee and General Gist was unable to arrange a meeting, instead mailing Governor Gist's letter with a cover letter of his own to chief executive M.S. Perry. Governor Perry's reply of November 9, Lincoln's election now a fact, was the boldest of all: "Florida may be unwilling to subject herself to the charge of temerity or immodesty by leading off, but will most assuredly cooperate with or follow the lead of any single Cotton State which may secede." Perry concluded, "If there is sufficient manliness at the South to strike for our rights, honor, and safety, in God's name let it be done before the inauguration of Lincoln."

From his cousin's diplomatic mission and other sources, Governor Gist was now armed with assurances that should South Carolina step out, at least part of Dixie would fall in line behind her. It was only logical that John C. Calhoun's Palmetto State go first. Here disunionism was far advanced, the public profoundly influenced by thirty years of education and argument from Southern rights groups, newspapers, teachers, preachers and politicians.

The South Carolina General Assembly gathered on November 5. When Lincoln emerged victorious as expected, house and senate voted unanimously for a "sovereignty convention" to be elected on December 6 and to assemble on December 17 for the purpose of dissolving South Carolina's ties with the Union. General Gist was back in Columbia and on hand to read the Governor's November 8 message to the legislature. Identified in the records as "S.R. Gist, Esq., his private secretary" he also delivered the Governor's important address of November 27 to a joint session. "It is gratifying to know that in the contemplated movement South Carolina has strong assurances that we will not stand alone..."[8] As he read the Governor's words to the assembled lawmakers States Rights Gist could take satisfaction in the part he had played, albeit secretly, in the course of events. Confidence that other states would follow made secession a certainty.

On December 7, ten days before the expiration of his term in office, South Carolina's Secession Governor made his parting remarks to the General Assembly: "I trust...that by the 25th of December no flag but the Palmetto will float over any part of South Carolina."[9]

Never before or since have South Carolinians displayed such unity of purpose. In Charleston on December 20 all 169 convention delegates voted for independence, igniting an explosion of unrestrained rejoicing.

Benjamin F. Perry was downcast and apprehensive. One of South Carolina's distinguished handful of unionists, Perry was a veteran of the losing battle over nullification and had fought to the bitter end against secession. However, "Our country is emphatically South Carolina first," and he would go with his state. Perry had friends among the most fiery of secessionists, including States Rights Gist, a young man he admired highly for his "character and talents." Whatever the future held, he was certain Gist would be in the forefront of the struggle.[10]

Chapter Five

"Young Men Are Dying to Fight For It"

Defiantly from the mountains to the sea, as in Governor's Gist's vision, flew the palmetto-and-crescent-emblazoned banners of the Republic of South Carolina. But from four sites in and near Charleston the Stars and Stripes of the Union still snapped in the breeze. All attention turned to these surviving outposts of Federal authority in secession's birthplace.

Major Robert Anderson commanded the small garrison of United States troops headquartered in Fort Moultrie on Sullivan's Island. He was also responsible for an obsolete harbor fortification called Castle Pinckney, imposing yet incomplete Fort Sumter, and the Charleston Arsenal that supplied these strongholds. South Carolina's declaration of independence put him in a most delicate position militarily and politically. He had a duty to perform. Yet Carolinians naturally looked on him and his men as a foreign military presence on the sacred soil of their homeland, a challenge to their freedom and honor.

A three-man commission, including former Governor Adams, journeyed to Washington to negotiate a transfer, with payment, of Fort Sumter and other Federal property to state control. Recovering from the initial shock over South Carolina's withdrawal, President James Buchanan, in the waning weeks of his presidency, grimly determined neither to recognize the legality of secession nor begin a war over it. To minimize the possibility of confrontation, he arrived at a gentlemen's agreement with then-Governor Gist that there be no change in the status of the Federal forces in Charleston harbor. For his part, Gist promised that state troops would not move against the Federal installations pending the outcome of negotiations.

Major Anderson was left in the dark. The last orders he received authorized him to defend himself if attacked and to use his own judgment in choosing a position. In great secrecy on the night of December 26 he did just that, transferring his command by boat from indefensible old Fort Moultrie to the island bastion of Fort Sumter. Cut off from land and secure behind Sumter's sixty-foot-tall brick walls, his defensive position was vastly improved. Though the fort was still under construction and not fully armed, Anderson's guns now completely dominated the harbor entrance, threatening the very spires of Charleston.

Justified militarily, from a political standpoint the move was precipitate. President Buchanan immediately denied any responsibility or knowledge of the Major's actions, though he balked at ordering him back. Newly-elected Governor Francis W. Pickens demanded that Anderson return, and when he refused the Governor ordered seizure of the remaining Federal forts.

He called to active duty the well-trained 4th Brigade of the South Carolina Militia. Late afternoon December 27 three local companies were ordered to take Castle Pinckney, the island fort off Charleston's battery. Expecting a fight, the handsomely-uniformed militiamen leaped from the deck of the guardboat *Nina* and charged up the dock. They were met by the protesting officer in charge, the only military man remaining. Just after dark the paddlewheeler *General Clinch* joined the *Nina* in transferring some 225 artillerymen armed as riflemen across the harbor to assault Fort Moultrie. Again they found no defenders and took possession without firing a shot.

The Federal Arsenal in the city had been surrounded by militia troops since mid-November, ostensibly for its own protection. On December 30 South Carolina infantrymen marched in, allowing the Federal commander to fire a 32-gun salute as he lowered his flag, one for each state still in the Union. The only remaining United States flag in South Carolina now flew on the parade ground of Fort Sumter.

On the eve of South Carolina's bid for independence, the 1860 Association, a group dedicated to secession, published a pamphlet that beat the drum for military preparedness. The author pointed out that technological advances, such as long-range artillery and improved small arms, were revolutionizing the art of war. Never before had the skill of the individual soldier been more crucial. "Taking these things into consideration," he concluded, "the people of the Southern States may be pronounced to be, in a miltary sense, unarmed; the militia, as at present organized and armed, serving only to generate a false security in the midst of danger."[1] A few militia organizations, such as the 4th and 9th Brigades, were as well-trained and equipped as could be expected of a part-time force. Still, the 1860 Association's sober assessment of reality was finally accepted by those in authority. If the Yankees decided on coercion, South Carolina would need an army permanently under arms.

As early as December 17, 1860 the General Assembly passed "An Act to Provide an Armed Military Force." The governor was authorized and required to receive volunteers out of the existing militia formations for twelve-month service. Each infantry battalion would send one company; two from each brigade. Already-established volunteer units that came forward would be permitted to enter the service as a group. Cavalry and artillery companies would likewise be received out of the regiments of the militia. Volunteers were to be armed and equipped by the state and reorganized into battalions, regiments and brigades. Company and field-grade officers would be elected, generals appointed by the governor and confirmed by the senate. Commanded by a major general, the Volunteer Forces of South Carolina would constitute one division of about 10,000 men.[2]

The sudden crisis brought on by Anderson's move to Fort Sumter put Governor Pickens on the spot. Mobilization of volunteers was just getting under way. The only fighting men at his disposal were the overburdened militiamen of Charleston's 4th Brigade, commanded by James Simons. To meet the emergency the Governor appealed to the still-assembled Secession Convention for authority to enlist volunteers immediately. In early January the Convention gave him authority, and considerable leeway, in raising a volunteer force under a six-month enlistment. Within a week Pickens had one regiment under arms: The 1st South Carolina Volunteers commanded by Colonel Maxcy Gregg.[3] On January 28 the legislature went one step further, creating a Regular Army of South Carolina. Officers of the new establishment would be appointed by the governor with the advice and consent of the senate, and enlisted men would serve for three years. Under this act the Governor put in the field an additional regiment of infantry, one battalion of artillery and a squadron of cavalry.[4] Supporting these proliferating military formations was a Corps of Engineers, authorized by the legislature January 26, 1861; and an Ordnance Bureau already established by the lawmakers November 13, 1860.[5]

South Carolina constitutionalists would be quick to deny that any revolution was in progress, since strictly-speaking "sovereigns cannot rebel." Yet in severing ties with the Union the Palmetto State's governmental structure went swiftly through chaotic transformations. In a sense the state had two governing bodies. The regularly elected house and senate represented their constituents, but the Secession Convention exercised the very sovereignty of the people "in convention assembled." The problem was more than academic. Bewilderment was so prevalent that the Adjutant and Inspector General found it necessary to publish a notice statewide explaining that the Convention's raising of troops "was designed to aid and not to supersede" the General Assembly's. Still, the Palmetto State in the chaos of mobilization ended up with three different infantry regiments, each bearing the proud title "1st South Carolina."[6]

Nowhere was confusion more apparent than in the office of the Adjutant and Inspector General. Elected by the legislature to a four-year term, at secession the office was held by Brigadier General Robert Gill Mills Dunovant. Under the provisions of the 1851 Militia Law he was "charged with the marshaling and inspection of troops, the correspondence in relation to all military affairs, and when in the field, with all general details of service of every description..." In former times record-keeping, reports and riding proudly in reviews were the extent of his duties. With the formation of the Ordnance Bureau in November 1860 his responsibilities were expanded to include service on the board that was to secure for the state arms and munitions.[7]

At the peak of the crisis over Major Anderson's taking refuge in Fort Sumter, Governor Pickens temporarily lost the services of his general on the scene. James Simons, commander of the 4th Militia Brigade, departed for Columbia to take up his other duties as speaker of the House of Representatives. In a move of questionable legality, on January 2 Governor Pickens turned over command of the brigade to General Dunovant. Nor was there statutory provision for filling Dunovant's now-vacant post. But these were unprecedented times and the Governor took responsibility for naming States Rights Gist Acting Adjutant and Inspector General of South Carolina. For a few weeks confusion reigned as orders and notices were issued alternately in Dunovant's and Gist's names. Finally by the middle of January General Gist dropped the "acting" from his title. At the end of the month Speaker Simons was back to resume his military role and General Dunovant simultaneously took command of the newly-created Regular Army of South Carolina. Gist's temporary job had become permanent. From the Executive Office of the Governor on January 29, 1861 came the orders: "States R. Gist having been appointed and commissioned Adjutant and Inspector General of the State of S.C....will be obeyed and respected accordingly."[8] Not for a year would the legislature again be in session and able to make their own choice. In the meantime there was work to be done: the herculean task of securing with the sword the independence South Carolinians demanded. As General Gist set up his headquarters in Charleston the eyes of the world turned to the city and her nearby forts.

Adjutant and Inspector General States Rights Gist posed for a Charleston photographer wearing the blue uniform of the South Carolina Militia.

(Museum of the Confederacy, Richmond)

The first test came almost immediately. The vacillating Buchanan administration finally made an effort to resupply and reinforce Anderson's garrison. A merchant ship called the *Star of the West* was chartered in New York, loaded with supplies and 200 troops and dispatched in supposed secrecy. Newspapers learned of the expedition and quickly the alarm was telegraphed to South Carolina. Out of range of Sumter's guns and commanding the main ship channel was the Morris Island Battery, manned by cadets of the South Carolina Military Academy. Arriving off Charleston in darkness the sidewheeler made her run toward Fort Sumter at daybreak January 9, preceded by a state guardboat firing rockets to alert the cadets. When the Yankee ship ignored a warning shot across her bow the teenaged gunners redirected their aim. Two hits were scored before the vessel retreated.

Major Anderson stood by his guns in angry and frustrated silence. The United States flag had been fired on for the first time. The offending cannon were beyond his range, but the Major could have begun the war then and there by lashing out at Fort Moultrie. Instead, he sent a heated protest to Governor Pickens threatening to sink all merchant ships that came in the port. Pickens coolly replied that South Carolina was no longer part of Anderson's United States. Not only did the Major have no right to remain in Sumter, but any attempt at reinforcement would be considered hostile and similarly repulsed.

The Union that Anderson was sworn to defend was rapidly unraveling. The day the *Star of the West* was fired upon, Mississippi declared her independence. On the tenth Florida seceded, followed by Alabama on the eleventh. Circumstances, to Governor Pickens, seemed right for negotiation. South Carolina Secretary of War David F. Jamison and Secretary of State Andrew G. Magrath met with Anderson and though he refused to abandon his post, an unofficial truce settled over the harbor. South Carolina's military would have time to prepare for the coming showdown.

Four stone-laden hulks were sunk in the main ship channel to impede the largest Federal men-of-war. South Carolina's little navy was doubled in size with the acquisition of the *Aid* and *Marion,* and construction began on an armor-plated floating battery. Gun emplacements constructed at old Fort Johnson and on Morris Island increased the firepower surrounding Anderson's garrison. From all over the state volunteers were rallying to Charleston; men who had to be armed, provisioned and assigned to their stations. For General Gist there were endless conferences with the Governor's Executive Council on such matters as progress of the work at the fortifications and procurement of munitions.[9]

No peacetime militia muster could ever train a man for this. Couriers brought messages to the Commander-in-

Chief's headquarters where Gist's office was identified by a paper sign pasted on the door. Orders for strengthening Fort Moultrie were delayed, complained one officer, by a shortage of laborers. Over on Sullivan's Island, Major Walter Gwynn of the Engineers feuded with Colonel Roswell S. Ripley and appealed to Gist. (The Major insisted that he took orders directly from the South Carolina War Department, not Ripley, and "I shall most certainly obey none of his orders.") There followed more complaints that General Dunovant was interfering with the construction work. An Adjutant and Inspector General neither planned strategy nor commanded troops in the field, but from the Governor to the men in the batteries every link in the newly-forged chain of command looked to Gist for coherence and order.[10]

By February, Georgia, Louisiana and Texas had joined the secession parade and delegates from the seven independent states were meeting in Montgomery, Alabama to form a new government. On the eighth a constitution was adopted and ten days later Jefferson Davis took the oath of office as President of the Confederate States of America. For Pickens, it was a matter of pride to resolve the Sumter standoff before the new authorities took responsibility away from him. On the sixth he issued orders to prepare for attack but was dissuaded by messages from the Montgomery delegates and a

Francis W. Pickens, controversial South Carolina Governor, 1860-1862. *(Century)*

telegraphic appeal for caution from sympathetic former-President John Tyler. The Governor was torn between a desire to take Sumter and fear of the consequences if he tried. Even if successful, he might be blamed for starting a war. At the end of February, President Davis ordered Major William Henry Chase Whiting, a professional soldier and engineer, to inspect the fortifications. The West Pointer was sharply critical and declared the batteries unready, but Pickens' belligerence had if nothing else stirred the President to action. "This Government assumes control of the military operations at Charleston...An officer goes tonight to take charge."[11] The Palmetto State's season of independence was over.

Native of Louisiana and U.S. Military Academy graduate, Pierre Gustave Toutant Beauregard was the ideal choice to command at Charleston. He made no immediate changes in the disposition of the troops and guns, but gradually and diplomatically corrected deficiencies. As all of his troops were South Carolinians, the Confederate commander was in daily contact with the state's Adjutant and Inspector General. Beauregard was impressed with Gist's efficiency and professionalism as he relied on the young man to marshal his forces. He would later commend the South Carolinian's "valuable assistance in obtaining and dispatching the troops for the attack on Fort Sumter and defense of the batteries."[12]

By now Lincoln was in office, and time was running out. Anderson by mid-April would have to capitulate for lack of food, ending the crisis at Fort Sumter. To force his way into the harbor with reinforcements and munitions would expose Lincoln to charges of aggression and probably fail anyway, so on April 8 the President informed Governor Pickens that an attempt would be made to bring supplies only to Sumter, confident this news would force the secessionists to attack before the arrival of the Federal fleet, thus placing the burden of starting the war on the South. Southerners felt they had little choice left, that in taking Sumter they were defending their country against the machinations of a hostile power, firm in a belief that "the aggressor in a war (that is, he who begins it) is not the *first* who *uses force*, but the first who renders force *necessary.*"[13]

Final preparations went ahead quickly in Charleston. The forty-three guns and mortars were placed in readiness. Additional troops were called up. Secret orders from General Gist on April 6 commanded Colonel Joseph B. Kershaw to put his 2nd Regiment on alert; forty-eight hours later the Colonel was ordered to "repair without delay to Charleston in the shortest possible time." There would be 7,000 South Carolinians in position: manning the batteries, patrolling beaches on horseback or providing infantry support in the event of a Federal amphibious assault.[14]

Orders came to Beauregard from Montgomery: Demand surrender of the fort, and if refused, reduce it. When Anderson declined to capitulate, the mortar battery at Fort Johnson opened fire at 4:30 a.m., April 12; the signal for all other guns to commence firing. The badly outnumbered and outgunned Federals gallantly returned fire at dawn, to the cheers of their Confederate adversaries. All through the day crowds of civilians on roofs and thronging Charleston's waterfront observed the terrific bombardment. When darkness came, and with it rain, Beauregard expected the fleet to begin landing troops. Confederate defenders on Morris and Sullivan's Islands were kept on alert to meet a threat that never materialized.

Daylight April 13 revealed heavy damage to the Federal bastion, yet Anderson stubbornly refused to give up. Incendiary "hot shot" from Fort Moultrie ignited Sumter's barracks, previously thought fireproof, and spread rapidly until flames threatened the powder magazine. Choking from the smoke, the Major at 1:30 p.m. finally struck his colors and across the harbor the thunder of guns was stilled. The punishment had lasted thirty-three hours, wrecking the masonry-and-wood fort. Confederate positions, protected by earth, cotton bales and iron, suffered minimal damage. Miraculously, no one was killed on either side.

The garrison was allowed to fire a salute to their flag on Sunday, April 14 before being transported to the Yankee ships outside the harbor; the fleet whose threatened arrival had precipitated hostilities while staying clear throughout the fight.

Before nightfall Beauregard, Pickens and their staffs crossed the harbor to witness Southern possession of the fort. It was a scene Adjutant and Inspector General Gist could never forget. Amid cheers, cannon salutes and bell-ringing, the Stars and Bars of the seven-state Confederacy was raised beside the blue banner of the Palmetto State. There they would remain through four bloody years of conflict.

The fire was barely out at Sumter when Lincoln called for 75,000 volunteers to march against the seceded states, and Northerners rushed to arms to avenge the insult to their flag. Lincoln would later concede privately his satisfaction that the "failed" naval expedition had succeeded, as he expected, in advancing "the cause of the country."[15] Outraged by his threatened invasion, Virginia, Tennessee, Arkansas and North Carolina responded by joining the Confederacy and Southerners expected Missouri, Kentucky and Maryland to follow suit.

"Secession is the fashion here," wrote British journalist William Russell from Charleston. His dispatch neatly summed up the post-Sumter euphoria: "Young ladies sing for it; old ladies pray for it; young men are dying to fight for it; old men are ready to demonstrate it. The founder of the school was St. Calhoun. His pupils carry out their teaching in thunder and fire. States' Rights are displayed after its legitimate teaching, and the Palmetto flag and the red bars of the Confederacy are its exposition."[16]

It was springtime on Wyoming plantation and April's warmth and verdant glory seemed to mirror Nathaniel Gist's gratification. The political creed he championed, liberty secure in state sovereignty, had long ago won-over the land of his birth. Now in his eighty-sixth year, he witnessed secession's triumph from the Chesapeake Bay to the deserts of west Texas. A new day of freedom and prosperity was dawning for the people of the South. Especially proud he was that States, the young son on whom he pinned so much hope, stood in the vanguard of the cause.

Chapter Six
"I Knowed He Was a General"

All attention turned northward to Virginia as the young men of South Carolina rushed to the long-sought showdown with the Yankees. Most expected the struggle to be glorious and brief. Former Governor Gist predicted peace would follow two Southern victories.[1] Adjutant General Gist was busy at his tasks of equipping the volunteers, mustering them into Confederate service and ordering them on to the front. Enthusiasm was rampant and he experienced little difficulty in meeting quotas set by the Confederate government.[2]

But with militia units depleted and so many men leaving the state, Governor Pickens grew uneasy. On May 27 he had Gist order militia General James Simons to keep his 4th Brigade in readiness for "any emergencies that may arise during the summer." Reacting to the hardships and restrictions of being under orders, Simons handed Gist a letter of complaint aimed at the Governor. "We are in the midst of Revolution and War," Pickens replied, "and all must submit to greater calls upon their time..." He was right, but had made a serious mistake in leaning on the militia. Speaker of the House Simons, nicknamed "Hospital Jimmy" for his knack of avoiding hostile fire during the Fort Sumter bombardment, had political ambitions that came first. When he noisily resigned his commission in July the Governor could add another enemy to an already impressive collection. Gist, though his duties placed him in the center of the quarrel, wisely maintained a detached professionalism.[3]

A naval incident with far-reaching consequences briefly involved the Adjutant General. The *Savannah,* a tiny one-gun Confederate privateer, sailed from Charleston on June 3. She took a Yankee merchantman before she was herself captured by a warship of the Federal blockading fleet. President Davis authorized Gist to arrange for an exchange of Union prisoners for the officers and crew of the *Savannah.* The General communicated with the fleet off Charleston only to learn the prisoners had been transferred to New York. Jailed as "pirates," the men faced execution as Lincoln ostensibly regarded the war as an insurrection. When Davis sternly threatened to hang Union prisoners in retaliation, Lincoln backed down. In future, those captured in battle would be treated as prisoners of war.[4]

With Federal troops under General Irvin McDowell massing in northern Virginia, Gist felt the time was at hand to stand with those he had sent off to war. This might be the decisive battle, his only chance to participate. Temporary service with the army could be combined with official state business: He and the Governor were in the process of setting up two camps of instruction for recruits, and while Gist was in Richmond, the new Confederate capital, he would meet with Secretary of War Leroy P. Walker and work out the details. In a letter that preceded his Adjutant, Pickens made the introduction: "General Gist will have a full interview with you, and he is fully acquainted with my views. You will find him a thorough-bred and accomplished officer of great information."[5]

Leaving his office in the hands of assistant Charles H. Simonton, Gist boarded the train for Richmond. At the War Department he conferred with Secretary Walker and quickly reported by mail to his Governor the results of the meeting. Perhaps commended by South Carolina's former U.S. Senator James Chesnut, Jr., Gist also had an audience with the President. An old friend and confidant of the chief executive, Chesnut was to play a critical and controversial role in Gist's career. On July 10 President Davis wrote General Joseph E. Johnston, commanding at Winchester: "General Gist, the adjutant-general of South Carolina, goes to your headquarters to make himself useful to you in any way he can serve you, and it gives me pleasure to commend him to your polite attention."[6]

Johnston assigned Gist to professional soldier and Mexican War veteran Barnard Elliott Bee of South Carolina. An awkward situation was gracefully averted when Brigadier General Gist temporarily shed his state rank to serve on Brigadier General Bee's staff in the uniform of a Confederate colonel.[7]

Guarding the Shenandoah Valley, Johnston commanded a force of 11,000, while to the east near Manassas 23,000 Confederates under Beauregard established a defensive line behind a stream called Bull Run. Beauregard was threatened by upwards of 35,000 soldiers under McDowell, up until that time the largest army ever assembled in American history. To make matters worse, Union reinforcements from the Valley were expected at any moment. The Confederates knew they must consolidate. On July 20 Johnston and a portion of his command joined Beauregard's army. Bee's brigade arrived around noon after a fifty-mile journey by rail, and went into reserve position.

Thus strengthened, Beauregard issued orders for his right wing to attack next day. Before he could make his move, early on the morning of July 21 McDowell launched a powerful and unexpected assault on the Confederate left. The Southern commander countered by ordering his reserves to the point of danger. Arriving first on the scene, General Bee immediately threw his regiments (the 4th Alabama, 2nd Mississippi and part of the 11th Mississippi) into the desperate fight. Aided by the arrival of Colonel Francis S. Bartow's Georgians, the men traded deadly volleys with the enemy. At 10:30 a.m. Bee ordered a charge that succeeded

only in devastating his brigade. Under intense counter-
assaults the embattled secessionists fell back. Disaster was
averted by the arrival of Colonel Wade Hampton's South
Carolina Legion and General Thomas Jonathan Jackson's
brigade of Virginians. Rallying his men, General Bee fell mortally wounded. By now convinced the battle would be decided
there on Henry Hill, Generals Beauregard and Johnston rode
to the sound of the guns.

Colonel Gist had helped the outnumbered Southern
troops meet and blunt the Union threat, in their sacrifice saving Beauregard's army from destruction. Now the battered
survivors staggered in confused disorder, with no one officer
commanding the field. Of Bee's men only the 4th Alabama
retained any coherence. To the rear and out of action, with
nearly all their officers killed or wounded, the Alabamians
stood at order-arms.

Galloping to the chaotic front, Beauregard's and
Johnston's first priority was to re-form the broken units and
stabilize the line. There was no outright panic, yet despite
their efforts the unsteady infantry simply would not hold
together. Disaster loomed. The generals then came upon the
leaderless 4th Alabama and Johnston called to his side their
regimental flag bearer. Beauregard spotted Colonel Gist, "a
young man whom I had known as adjutant general of South
Carolina, and whom I greatly esteemed," and placed him in
command of the regiment. With a cheer the Alabamians
followed their flag forward, and around these stalwart soldiers
and Jackson's Virginians, the front was restored. Colonel Gist
would remain in command of the gallant regiment the remainder of the day.[8]

Beauregard by 2 p.m. felt strong enough to order an advance, but the Federals were pushed from the field only to
counterattack and regain their lost ground. Further reinforced, Beauregard again sent the Southern line forward, taking heavy casualties while regaining the plateau. Gist was
wounded leading his regiment.[9]

Out of the southwest appeared a column of approaching troops. Squinting through his field glasses, Beauregard strained to make identification as a summer breeze unfurled their battle banner. Anxiety turned to exultation as he beheld the Stars and Bars! It was the brigade of Colonel Jubal Anderson Early, last of the South's Valley reinforcements. As Early's men moved into position, the thrilling news of their arrival spread among the weary troops. With Rebel yells the Confederates surged forward. The Federals wavered — then broke — then scattered in panic.[10]

What remained of Bee's brigade was too exhausted to pursue the routed enemy. Gist could be thankful he had survived his baptism of fire, done his duty and seen the day close in victory. Unable to deliver the death-blow to their adversaries and end the war, the triumphant Southerners had at least removed the immediate threat. The capital was safe.

Gist repaired to Richmond and there tarried through August, recovering from his injuries and nurturing his social and political connections. Prominent among his influential allies was Senator Chesnut. Chesnut was serving in the provisional Confederate Congress (a unicameral body), but expected soon to represent South Carolina for a full six-year term as Senator under the permanent Constitution. He and Gist may have known each other in the years before secession, and as they now became better acquainted, their mutual respect grew. Mary Chesnut, the Senator's wife and famed diarist, recorded meeting the General, mildly surprised to discover that States Rights Gist "is a real personage — and not an odd name merely..."[11]

Gist soon felt the need to return home and resume his responsibilities. Back in Columbia, Acting Adjutant General Simonton had fallen into an annoying habit of dropping the "Acting" from his title.[12] More ominously, there were indications that a Union attack was being aimed at South Carolina.

The Palmetto State's long coastline was vulnerable to assault from an enemy who enjoyed complete naval supremacy. General Gist and others frankly expected some sort of invasion by winter, but where would the enemy strike? The territory to be defended was a maze of barrier islands and tidal creeks. The lack of vast numbers of troops supported by artillery made complete security from invasion unrealistic. With hostile armies everywhere pressing the borders of the country, Confederate authorities had few resources for South Carolina. Governor Pickens and his Adjutant General would engage Richmond in a tug-of-war over troops remaining in the state, Gist arguing that South Carolina had done her share for Virginia and now needed to hold on to soldiers still at home.[13]

Port Royal Sound, between Charleston and Savannah, was the most likely Union objective and it was here Confederate defenders concentrated their meager resources. Preparations were to prove woefully inadequate. In October of 1861 a Federal invasion fleet of unprecedented strength was ordered south to a rendezvous at Port Royal. Fifteen powerful warships escorted thirty-six transports loaded with 12,653 blue-clad soldiers. On November 7, the 148 guns of the fleet pounded the brave but hopelessly outnumbered and outgunned defenders. In a few hours it was over. The Federals had won their first great victory of the war, gaining a strategic foothold in the state where secession began.

Stepping from the train in Charleston, on the very day of the Port Royal assault, was the new Confederate commander of South Carolina, Georgia and Eastern Florida: handsome Virginian, Robert E. Lee. Fortunately, the enemy were reluctant to advance inland, and Lee took advantage of their inactivity to speed building of defenses at Charleston, Savannah and along the railroad that linked the two cities. His efforts were hampered by chronic shortages of men and guns. In a letter to Secretary of War Judah P. Benjamin on December 3, Lee complained of South Carolina's "languid" response to the invasion of her soil. Recruits in large numbers were simply not coming forward from the manpower remaining in the state.[14]

A jumbled chain of command had state troops under Lee subject at times to conflicting orders. Gist was disturbed when reports of these irregularities reached him in Columbia. On December 12 he promised Lee that "The troops of the State are entirely without any reservation under your control..." He pledged "the most hearty and sincere cooperation" of South Carolina authorities in carrying out Lee's orders. "Permit me to add that they do this the more cheerfully," wrote the admiring Gist, "as you possess their entire confidence." In reply, Lee thanked Gist for "this fresh assurance of your kindness and consideration," adding that he felt "deeply obliged at your placing the troops of the State under my command."[15]

Gist himself had just received a vote of confidence in the handling of his office, the position he had held under appointment for eleven months. On November 28, the South Carolina House and Senate met in joint session to ballot for Adjutant and Inspector General, and Gist was elected without apparent opposition.[16]

Soon after the legislature's action Gist learned that his father was seriously ill and hastened to his side. Nathaniel Gist died at Wyoming on December 3. "Ardently devoted to the welfare of his beloved country," eulogized Pastor Saye, "he manifested a deep interest in the success of the Revolution in which we are now engaged." Two years previous the old man had found peace in the faith that sustained Elizabeth.[17]

While General Gist gathered with his family on the plantation, Senator Chesnut was surprisingly defeated by a vote of the legislature for a seat in the Confederate Senate. A bitterly disappointed Mary Chesnut felt that the Senator's friends in and out of the General Assembly could have used their influence on her husband's behalf, but were themselves unaware of the impending challenge. "General Gist, for whom Mr. C. had done so much, had to go to his ill father. None of them knew the election was coming off or that there was any opposition."[18] President Davis would miss his friend's counsel and support in Congress. As it turned out, Chesnut's return to his troubled state came at a critical time.

For months, discontent had been building against Governor Pickens. His administration was perceived as failing to provide firm leadership in the face of war and invasion. As early as September 18 General Gist could close a letter to the War Secretary with the remarkably revealing statement that "The Governor being absent, I am temporarily in charge of State matters." To fill the leadership vacuum, the Secession Convention (still acting in the name of the people) created a new Executive Council with virtually unlimited authority. This would be no advisory body. The Governor himself would merely serve as one of five members; the 'others being Lieutenant Governor William Wallace Harlee, Attorney General Isaac William Hayne, former Governor William H. Gist and former Senator James Chesnut, Jr.[19]

Meeting on January 9, 1862, Chesnut took on the crucial responsibility of heading up the Executive Council's Department of the Military. In effect, Chesnut superseded the Governor as commander-in-chief. One of his first orders was to require the bureaus under his jurisdiction to report. Adjutant and Inspector General Gist responded with a statement showing that on January 1, 1862 South Carolina had 27,362 men in the field. Some four-thousand were militiamen on active duty; the rest in Confederate service. Of those in the Confederate army however, only a fraction had

James Chesnut, Jr. His political influence gave States Rights Gist the boost he needed.
(South Caroliniana Library)

volunteered for the duration of the war. Most were sworn-in for shorter periods and thousands of enlistments were about to expire. With half of its former members in Confederate gray, the old militia was, in Chesnut's words, "virtually disorganized."[20]

Gone too was the former image of the State Adjutant and Inspector General. The antebellum functionary decked-out in blue-uniformed elegance had been replaced by the hard-driven agent of a revolutionary government. There were numberless meetings with the Council, and conferences with Lee and other military men. Training centers had to be organized in St. Andrew's Parish outside Charleston and at Lightwood Knot Springs near Columbia. Workshops were needed for repairing small arms. Long, tedious hours were spent on reports and plans and correspondence. Gist may have preferred active service with his comrades at the front, but his mobilization work was at this point invaluable to the Southern cause.[21]

His greatest challenge came on February 2 when the Confederacy asked the state to fill a quota of 18,000 troops sworn-in for the war. Lest South Carolina fall short, every man already in service for a shorter period must re-enlist for the duration, plus five new regiments had to be raised. Gist prepared, under Chesnut's direction and the Council's mandate, a plan for a military draft in South Carolina. The Council approved, and put the measure into effect March 7 with widespread publicity. While 5,000 volunteers were called for, notice was given that on March 20 volunteering would end and conscription of eighteen to forty-five year-olds begin. No individual or volunteer company would be permitted to enter Confederate service except "for the war unconditionally." Those who failed to register in the first ten days would be drafted first, and Sheriffs and tax collectors were required to aid in the enrollment. The Council delegated considerable authority to the Adjutant General, at whose discretion "essential" employees of factories and overseers of plantations could receive certificates of exemption. "All arms-bearing men should be ordered to the field before it is too late to organize," concluded Gist. "We have waited long enough."[22]

As it turned out, Gist's plan was so successful that the state draft was unnecessary. Faced with the disgrace of becoming draftees, over four-thousand more volunteers than were called for came forward. A month later the Confederate Congress passed its own version of conscription, superseding South Carolina's, and the response was again favorable. To its credit, the Executive Council exercised vast powers with responsibility and restraint. Most important, they and the Adjutant General succeeded admirably in their primary task of mobilizing the state. In the course of the war an estimated 60,000 South Carolinians would fight under the Confederate flag.[23]

Even those few South Carolinians who opposed secession now unreservedly supported the Confederate cause. From Greenville, Benjamin Perry condemned the United States for "trying to reverse the principles announced in the American Declaration of Independence and their attempt to subvert the basis of self government by our subjugation..." The former unionist denounced Lincoln's war as "the most diabolical national crime ever committed by a civilized and Christian people."[24]

The conflict was about to enter its second year, and Gist had for some time been chafing to leave his desk and return to the army. He understood better than most the importance of his work, but in his heart he knew the war was going to be won on the battlefield, not in a Columbia office. Yet his position itself presented a problem. It would be humiliating to step down in rank to command in the field, when he had for so many years worn the stars of a South Carolina general officer. He coveted nothing less than a Confederate brigadier's commission.

President Davis, like his counterpart Abraham Lincoln, was under constant pressure to make military appointments based on political considerations. It was tempting to repay debts with a uniform. Even a man of Davis' rigid principles understood political reality. If a commission was to be had, Gist surely reasoned, Chesnut's open door to the chief executive was his best hope.

For his part, Chesnut saw in Gist genuine ability and commitment and felt justified in staking his reputation on the young man. There is evidence that Chesnut wrote directly to the President recommending Gist's appointment, implying intentionally or not, that he spoke for the entire Executive Council. We know that on March 14 Chesnut mailed a carefully-worded letter to his friend William Porcher Miles, South Carolina Congressman and Chairman of the powerful Military Affairs Committee of the Confederate House of Representatives.

> It is more than probable that my friend Genl. S.R. Gist[,] Adj. Genl. of the state[,] will be urged by his friends for the appointment of Brigadier Genl. in the Provisional Army: I could speak of him & his qualifications in the highest & sincerest terms; but to you who know him it is unnecessary. I invoke your aid to enlist our Delegation in his behalf, and to present him to the President. No better appointment from this state could, in my opinion, be possibly made.

With the endorsement of his trusted friend Chesnut, and the apparent backing of the state's leadership, Davis on March 19 sent Gist's name to the Senate, where next day the nomination was routinely confirmed. States Rights Gist had won the gold wreath and stars of a Confederate brigadier general.[25]

Congratulations came from all sides, and he gloried in his new status. The day the newspapers announced his commission he took a room in the Congaree House Hotel in Columbia and there ran into Mary Chesnut. Toward his benefactor's wife he exhibited "modest complaisance." Later Mrs. Chesnut recorded the revealing observation of her servant.

States Rights Gist, newly-commissioned Confederate Brigadier General. The *carte de visite* was made in Columbia, probably in March, 1862. *(South Caroliniana Library)*

" 'I knowed he was a general,' said Maum Mary, as he passed by. 'He told me as soon as he got in his room befo' his boy put down his trunk!' "[26]

Even before considering the appointment of staff officers, the new General wisely selected Wiley Howard to be his personal servant. They had been friends since childhood days onWyoming plantation, and Wiley, like his master, knew and loved horses. Before the war he was Nathaniel Gist's coachman, on occasion driving family members to distant vacation spots in North Carolina and Virginia. Described as "a man of unusual ability and character," Wiley would prove the ideal choice to accompany Gist to duty in the field.[27]

The President had just summoned Lee back to Virginia. Major General John C. Pemberton, West Point graduate and professional soldier, was the new Confederate commander on the coast. Perhaps reasoning that Gist's South Carolina understanding and perspective would be helpful to the Northern-born Pemberton, the War Department on April 8 ordered the newly-minted brigadier to Charleston. An assignment within South Carolina was welcome news to Gist and smoothed his transition from state to Confederate service.[28]

"The whole military formation of the State had to pass through his hands," acknowledged the *Charleston Mercury.* Reviewing Gist's career as Adjutant and Inspector General, the editor reminded his readers that he "discharged the extremely laborious and the difficult duties of his office with both ability and fidelity." The future looked bright indeed. "We are satisified that if a cool head, courage and energy can achieve for him more honor in the field, and fresh services to his State, he will win the one and perform the other."[29]

Chapter Seven
"He is the Junior and Obeys Orders Only"

Executive Council responsibilities demanded much from Gist. Yet work in Columbia was not without recompense, as a short ride from the city dwelt a certain young lady. Everyone called her Janie. Christened Jane Margaret after her mother, she was born June 26, 1841, daughter of James Hopkins Adams. A child of one of South Carolina's wealthiest families, she lived with her parents at magnificent Live Oak Plantation in the Congaree section of lower Richland District.[1]

Educated at Yale, James Hopkins Adams was an early convert to the cause of states' rights. Membership in the Nullification Convention of 1832-1833 was followed by four terms in the South Carolina House of Representatives and two in the State Senate. For as long as Janie could remember, the Gists had been family friends. William H. Gist and Joseph Gist served with her father in the General Assembly, where together they championed state sovereignty and finally secession. Adams was elected governor in 1854, and on trips to the upcountry was entertained in the parlor of Nathaniel Gist's Wyoming.[2]

As a teenager Janie with her family made a grand tour of Europe. According to gossip, the real purpose of the trip was to break up an unwelcome romance involving one of the Adams daughters and a mysterious "Mr. H." of Charleston. In any event, Janie survived the perils of adolescence. One who knew her from girlhood described the young belle as "accomplished" and "one of the most amiable and lovely of her sex."[3] She and States came from very similar backgrounds; both born to the privileges, prejudices and responsibilities of Palmetto aristocracy. It seemed a good match, despite their ten-year age difference.

Governor Adams had died while Gist was in Virginia and the prescribed period of mourning may have put a damper on wedding plans. Now in the euphoria of his promotion and anticipation of front-line duty there loomed a painful separation, though at some point an understanding was reached between the two.

He arrived in Charleston as another in a series of unwelcome troop transfers forced Pemberton to reorder his command. Gist went to work organizing a staff that would include Captains Joseph Walker and Carlos Tracy, and the General's younger brother, Lieutenant James D. Gist.[4] Pemberton was at first unsure where to use his new brigadier, though he hoped Gist could act as a "liaison" with the Executive Council as they attempted to influence placement of Confederate troops.[5]

There had been a tense moment near the end of the Council's May 13 meeting, though news of the episode probably never reached Gist. Benjamin F. Arthur, Gist's former law partner and now the Council's secretary, tersely kept the minutes. Lieutenant Governor Harlee read a letter he had received from General James Jones, Chairman of the Board of Visitors of the South Carolina Military Academy. According to the widely-connected Jones, "President Davis has stated the appointment of Gen. S.R. Gist as Brigadier General in the Confederate States service was on the recommendation of the Council..." Accusing eyes must have turned on the chagrined Chesnut, though his response went unrecorded. The Senator's colleagues would finally agree to a carefully-worded resolution they hoped would set the record straight without publicly striking a chord of disharmony. Their rebuke was aimed at Chesnut and not General Gist. They had no "complaint or objection to the action of the President in making the appointment." Still, members "deem it due to truth and justice to say that they have recommended no one for that office..."[6]

That same month Gist assumed command of "James Island and Dependencies," a jigsaw puzzle of real estate and key to Charleston's defenses.[7] On the coast the sand dunes of Morris and Folly Islands stood isolated by marshlands and accessible only by boat. James Island itself was bounded on the north by Charleston harbor, on the south and west by the Stono River and cut off from the rest of St. Andrew's Parish by Wappoo Creek.

Establishing his headquarters at Secessionville, Gist reported an aggregate strength of 3,925 officers and men. Secessionville was a cluster of James Island vacation cottages, apparently named in jest years before when several young couples chose to "secede" from their elders and summer there. The newest resident now got down to the business of strengthening fortifications, mounting guns, and consolidating his lines.[8]

Pemberton had had consolidation in mind back on March 27, when he abandoned tiny Cole's Island at the mouth of the Stono River. He was sure the batteries there were indefensible and ordered the guns relocated. In doing so he opened the Stono to Federal gunboats and made attack on Charleston through James Island likely. The move seriously eroded the Executive Council's confidence in Pemberton and soon evolved into a *cause célèbre* within the state.[9]

The Confederate commander had already given up without a fight "untenable" positions near Georgetown, and was toying with the idea of abandoning Forts Moultrie and Sumter and defending Charleston from the city itself. South

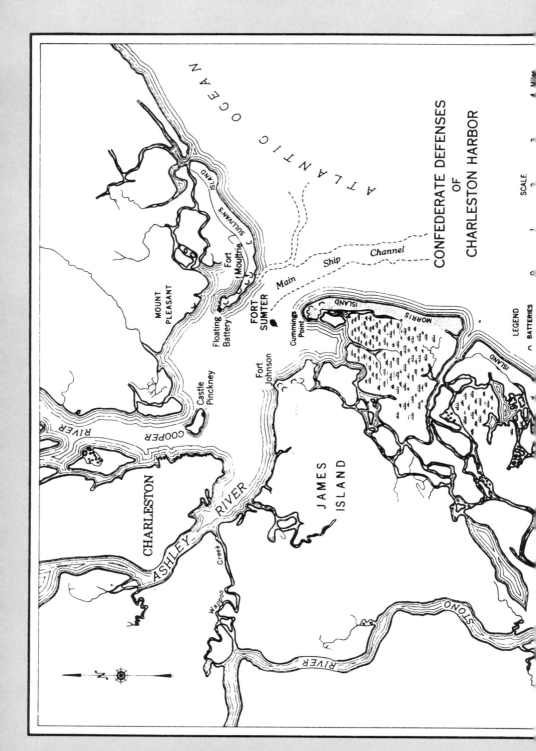

CHARLESTON, SOUTH CAROLINA
(National Park Service)

Carolina bristled with each retreat. A nervous Council resolved that Charleston "should be defended at any cost of life or property..." They hoped to stiffen Pemberton's backbone with unequivocal talk of preferring victory "with the entire city in ruins to an evacuation or surrender on any terms whatever." Lee himself urged Pemberton to battle for the city "street by street and house by house as long as we have a foot of ground to stand upon."[10] Her great seaport was essential to the Southern war effort; as spiritual capital of the Confederacy Charleston's value was incalculable.

Gist, unhappy over the Cole's Island pullback, was at least able to post two infantry companies there under Lieutenant Colonel Ellison Capers with orders to keep a lookout for approaching enemy gunboats. "Dummy" cannon were installed to "keep up appearances." The General's other forces made ready a line that stretched across James Island and took defensive advantage of every creek and marsh. Increased Yankee gunboat activity up the Stono made it clear an attack would not be long in coming.[11]

" 'Doom' hangs over wicked Charleston," blustered the New York *Tribune*. "That viper's nest and breeding place of rebellion is, ere this time, invested by Union Arms — perhaps already in our hands."[12]

On June 2 the Yankees began landing men at the southern end of James Island under cover of their gunboats. Other troops from occupied John's Island ferried across the river a little further upstream. Sharp skirmishing broke out in the no-man's-land between the armies, but indirect cannon fire from the river vessels, accurately directed by forward observers, discouraged effective Southern opposition. As they reconnoitered enemy positions Gist and his aides were on one occasion covered with sand by an exploding shell. Another projectile narrowly missed the General's headquarters. Gist's Confederates desperately prepared defenses while trying to guess when and where the blow would strike.[13]

At this juncture, Pemberton allowed his chain of command on James Island to become a tangle. On June 3 Brigadier General Hugh W. Mercer arrived from Savannah with reinforcements, replacing Gist as senior officer on the island. Three days later Brigadier General William Duncan Smith assumed command. He was replaced on June 14 by Brigadier General Nathan George "Shanks" Evans. "There were three different generals commanding in this short campaign," observed Colonel Johnson Hagood (not counting Mercer's brief tenure), "and as each one arrived he took charge of everything, holding the others in reserve as second and sometimes third in command. The fact is, things were pretty haphazard." All the generals were quartered together, "and there was considerable unpleasantness among them," Hagood reported, "as much perhaps from the anomalous relations in command which they held toward each other, as from any other cause."[14]

At least amid the disarray Secessionville's defenses were not neglected. Here water and impassable marsh made a narrow piece of high ground the only approach possible for an attacking force. Across this little peninsula, the Confederates hurriedly strengthened an earthen fort, construction going on nearly around the clock under the direction of Colonel Thomas G. Lamar.

At 3 a.m. on the morning of June 16, Lamar allowed his 500 exhausted men to sleep. Their brief rest almost proved disastrous. At dawn Confederate pickets were overwhelmed by attacking Unionists and barely succeeded in warning the fort. An invading force, 6,600 strong, meant to break through the Southern line at Secessionville and march on Charleston.

Lamar's guns, already loaded with grapeshot, thundered the alarm and cut bloody paths through the oncoming formations. The narrowness of the peninsula made it impossible for the Federals to maneuver or bring their full force to bear, but the disciplined blue ranks kept on coming. Lamar was himself severely wounded in fierce hand-to-hand combat atop the parapet. Gradually, Southern reinforcements began to arrive. Off to the right flank and across the marsh Lieutenant Colonel Ellison Capers, commanding two 24-pounder guns, helped shatter repeated Federal attacks. In all, the fighting lasted two and one-half hours until Northern commander Brigadier General Henry W. Benham finally ordered a retreat. Union dead, wounded and missing totaled about 700 compared to 200 Confederate casualties.

Looking for someone to blame, Yankee higher-ups had Benham arrested and sent North in disgrace. Southerners hailed the heroic Lamar and his gallant men. The Confederate Congress passed a resolution of thanks and the unnamed earthwork was afterwards called Fort Lamar in honor of the hard-fighting Colonel. It had not been an outstanding day for the high command on either side. Victory was won on the very parapet of Lamar's fort without the benefit of general officers. Third-in-command Gist apparently remained at headquarters with Pemberton directing reinforcements to the front until it was all over.[15]

Colonel Hagood had harsh words for "Shanks" Evans' failure to lead throughout the campaign, especially after June 15, when the General moved his headquarters four miles rearward to the shore overlooking Charleston harbor. Colonel Capers, in a letter to his wife just before the battle, complained of the "great deficiency" in generals. He respected

Ellison Capers, graduate of the South Carolina Military Academy, later Colonel of the 24th South Carolina Regiment.
(From Walter Capers, Soldier-Bishop)

Pemberton and Smith personally, though he thought them poor officers. But nothing could redeem the James Island commander. "Genl. Evans is a coward," charged the Colonel, "with a reputation for bravery which he has earned by sending his men and officers where he never dreams of going. He keeps himself out of range and gets away from fire whenever by chance he gets in it. He is reckless, without any judgement & terribly pompose [sic] & drinks to excess."

Only one superior completely escaped Capers' criticism: "Genl. Gist is cool, has a good head & I have great confidence in him," lauded the Colonel, "but he is the junior and obeys orders only, without originating them."[16]

Two days after the battle, with thousands of Union troops still very much a threat on James Island, Pemberton got around to restructuring his beefed-up command. Evans returned to the Second Military District south of the city. Smith received overall responsibility for James Island while Gist was assigned to command of the troops east of James Island Creek, largest and most important section of the district. On July 8 Smith's area of responsibility was expanded, and in turn the entire island's 8,579 Confederates were placed under Gist.[17]

Soon after the battle, Generals Gist and Smith made a personal reconnaissance outside the lines and found the enemy packed onto Battery Island under gunboat protection. The discovery forced Gist to cancel his half-formulated plan for a demonstration against the 9,000 Federals still on Charleston's doorstep. Numerically superior and supported by naval firepower, the Union army was unassailable.[18] Yet the new Yankee commander insisted that a renewed offensive on his part would be impossible without massive reinforcements. Withdrawal the only alternative, by July 9 the Federals had abandoned the island.

With the pressure off Charleston, Confederate authorities ordered Pemberton to send half his force to Richmond. Even after the subsequent organizational shake-up Gist emerged as commander of a 6,600 man force, the largest on the coast.[19]

The commanding general himself would be next to go. If his transfer was a concession to critics, Jefferson Davis demonstrated personal faith in Pemberton by assigning him to the President's home state of Mississippi. Governor Pickens was delighted. Not only was he rid of Pemberton; the General's replacement would be Beauregard, the still-popular Hero of Sumter. Gist too must have been glad to learn he would serve under his old chief.

Beauregard realized the coastal assignment was a demotion for a disappointing performance in the West and further embittered him against the President. Yet in Charleston the "Southern Napolean" would do much to redeem a clouded reputation, waging the kind of siege warfare that perfectly suited his talents. On September 25, the day after he formally assumed command, Beauregard sorted out the forces in the two states he defended. Georgia would be under a single officer; South Carolina's coast divided into three districts. Stretching from James Island to the North Carolina line and comprising 133 companies of infantry, artillery and cavalry was the First District. This, the largest and most important section of his command, Beauregard entrusted to his young friend Gist.[20]

For now the coast seemed unthreatened; the cooler temperatures of October welcomed with pageantry in the First District. "The review of the forces on James Island yesterday," reported the *Mercury* on October 10, "was quite an imposing military display." To many it probably called to mind old peacetime militia musters. The two-hour review began at 11 a.m. with the arrival of Generals Beauregard and Gist with their staffs. "At the close of the review, the field officers present assembled and were introduced [to Beauregard] by Brigadier General Gist." Next day was the navy's turn to show off, as the new ironclad *Palmetto State* received her christening. The two generals were present for the ceremony, arriving early with their entourage and taking a highly visible position on the upper deck.[21]

The pleasant lull was broken in late October by a Yankee attack in Johnson Hagood's district south of Charleston. This time the Federal objective was to cut the railroad at Pocataligo. Gist was ordered there with reinforcements, but before he arrived the newly-promoted General Hagood had already secured a victory[22]

In the daily routine of command, Gist was experiencing many of the same frustrations common to other Confederate generals in dealing with state authorities. No, answered the Executive Council on October 2, Gist could not remove houses on Sullivan's Island — only the governor had that authority and he cannot be reached. No, the state cannot afford to defend railroad bridges in the interior — that expense, answered Chesnut, would have to be borne by the railroad companies or the Confederate government. If Gist thought his friendship and former state position would prove a unique advantage in Confederate service he was abruptly introduced to reality.[23]

In the closing days of the Pickens administration, the chief executive's interference in Confederate military matters inadvertently cost Gist his new assignment. Pickens had written President Davis requesting the Governor's friend Roswell S. Ripley be returned to Charleston from Virginia. Hoping to appease the difficult Governor, Beauregard went along. Senior in date of rank, Brigadier General Ripley replaced Gist in the First District on October 16; Gist resuming command of "James Island and the Main."[24]

At least on the surface Gist took the demotion in good grace and a spirit of cooperation, and soon he and Ripley were working together. At Beauregard's request the two generals submitted an estimate of the forces they felt were needed to properly defend Charleston. What they proposed was a better than five-fold increase in manpower. Beauregard put his imprimatur on this exercise in wishful thinking, probably hoping Richmond might take it seriously and slow down their relentless requisition on his forces.[25]

The next call for help came not from Richmond but North Carolina. From their base at New Bern, the enemy had in December marched inland toward the railroad that connected Wilmington with Petersburg and the Confederate capital. A Federal fleet was also reported on the way. Brigadier General William H. C. Whiting, Southern commander at Wilmington, frantically telegraphed Beauregard for reinforcements. In response, Beauregard from his various commands gathered up a force of 5,000 men and three light batteries, organized as a division. Described by the General as "all excellent troops," he placed Gist in command and sent them north December 15.[26]

The feared attack never materialized and by the first of the year the men returned to South Carolina. "I send you this note by your able brigadier, General Gist," wrote the grateful Whiting to Beauregard. "I beg you will receive my true and real thanks for the promptness with which you sent your magnificent troops to my assistance at a time when it was thought they were needed."[27]

Quickly Gist reported on the brief Wilmington assignment, informing Beauregard that "delays were occasioned by overloading the trains, by the worn-out condition of the locomotives, want of wood and water at proper stations, and want of system in running the trains... I would respectfully suggest that the matter be examined into and that the evils be remedied..." Possibly in search of such a remedy, and certainly to secure greater cooperation between the two Carolina commands, Gist himself was ordered back to Wilmington with "such of his staff as he may need."[28]

Whiting, a career soldier, had requested the presence of lawyer-militiaman Gist. The two brigadiers came to their positions from paths as different as were their temperaments. Graduating first in the West Point class of 1845, Whiting earned the finest academic record up to that time. In dealing with superiors the Mississippian had a reputation for curtness if not insubordination, a failing that hurt him professionally despite his unquestioned ability. Whiting found in Gist a friend his equal intellectually. They could surely learn from each other. In a long letter to Beauregard on January 8, Whiting described his military situation and lamented Gist not having his troops with him as "we might trouble the enemy greatly." Nevertheless, "I am very much obliged for Gist. He is cool, sensible, and brave."[29]

Gist was not in North Carolina to serve as a mere adviser however. On January 6 he took command of a small division of North Carolinians and resolutely he set to work preparing them for action. There was much work to be done. Inspections that he ordered revealed "gross neglect" on the part of company officers in not insuring that arms were fit for service. Discipline and basic military courtesy were sadly lacking. One lieutenant colonel was absent without leave and other regimental officers "do not appear to be well versed in their duties." Changes must be made quickly. "Commanding officers," ordered Gist, "will minutely and thoroughly examine the arms and ammunition of their respective commands." Routine camp duty and drill "will be established and observed rigidly. Order and discipline must be strictly enforced." Looking beyond their problems, Gist sought to encourage one of his brigade commanders with the reminder that his troops "fight upon their native soil and in defense of their families, homes and firesides."[30]

Whiting continued to fret for the safety of his District of Cape Fear. Confederate Major General Gustavus Woodson Smith wrote Beauregard from Goldsborough, underlining the importance of keeping Wilmington out of Yankee hands. "They cannot take Wilmington by land, I think, if General Gist with the troops he had there before is in the place in time to maneuver in front and check their approach." Reluctantly, Beauregard was persuaded to act. "I send all forces I can spare from this department; same as before." And, as before, their stay was short as the anticipated attack never materialized. Soon word came that Beauregard himself was expecting trouble, and in the first week of February, Gist relinquished his temporary command and returned to the Palmetto State with Beauregard's troops.[31]

"I believe an attack on Charleston almost certain at an early day," warned the Confederate Secretary of War. Preparations went forward as the Yankees delayed. Gist was reassigned to James Island and St. Andrew's Parish and made his headquarters at the centrally-located McLeod Plantation. "In accordance with your written instructions," reported Gist to his immediate superior General Ripley, "I made a thorough personal inspection of the entire division..." He commanded a fundamentally well-planned and constructed network of breastworks and earthen forts mounting over sixty guns.[32]

Gist again recommended that Cole's Island be reoccupied and held. Lee, Pemberton, and now Beauregard all wrote-off the exposed island as indefensible, yet Gist steadfastly maintained that its abandonment had been a mistake. Recapture, he insisted, would clear the Stono of troublesome Yankee gunboats and permit a shortening of the Confederate lines on James Island. His theory would never be tested.[33]

In early March Gist again wrote to Ripley with strategic advice he hoped would be passed along to Beauregard. Sad experience with Southern railroads convinced Gist that converging forces at threatened points wasted precious time. "My suggestion was and is to concentrate troops and transportation at some proper point on the railroad or in Charleston...and be in readiness to move 5,000 men to any point in a few hours." Ripley forwarded the letter with his endorsement, but it made no impression on Beauregard: "The general commanding will be happy to have the opinions of his subordinate officers at the proper time."[34]

It seemed the proper time though for "Old Bory" to set Gist straight concerning the chain of command. In mid-February Ripley had apparently modified Gist's placement of troops within the James Island and St. Andrew's subdivision. Annoyed, Gist went over Ripley's head in bringing the matter to Beauregard. The commanding General's icy response should have been expected. "When General Ripley arrived here General Gist was ordered to report to him for duty. On General Gist's return from North Carolina he was again (verbally) ordered to report to General Ripley for the same duty..." In reordering Gist's troop dispositions and "correcting the error," Ripley was only doing his job.[35]

There is no evidence that ill-feeling lingered or affected Gist's performance. But Beauregard's chastening must have stung; all the more so being deserved. In mid-March the commander called together a board of Generals Ripley, Gist, and James H. Trapier to investigate and report on certain specific questions involving Charleston's defenses.[36] Beauregard's underlying purpose may have been simply to encourage a meeting of the minds among his brigadiers. Pemberton had allowed potentially disastrous confusion to reign on James Island just prior to the Battle of Secessionville. Old Bory would not repeat that mistake.

The long-delayed attack was imminent. What no one expected was the form it would take. The Northern army had been beaten at Charleston, now it was the navy's turn to show them how it was done. Yankee technology had fashioned a fleet of modern ironclad vessels armed with some of the most powerful ordnance in existence. According to plan, the 8-inch, 11-inch and 15-inch guns of the fleet would pound Forts Sumter and Moultrie into dust. The warships would then force their way into the harbor, making Charleston's surrender inevitable.

April 7 the seemingly invincible armada steamed to the attack as Fort Sumter's band defiantly struck up "Dixie." General Gist commanded the James Island troops from Fort Johnson on the harbor. His guns, part of the harbor's inner defenses, test-fired two shells but found they were out of range.[37] Confederate guns at the harbor entrance were unequal to those of the fleet, but the fire of the Rebel cannoneers was devastatingly intense and amazingly accurate. During the battle the Yankee ironclads were hit a total of 520 times, suffering substantial damage. The double-turreted *Keokuk* took terrific punishment and sank next morning. Admiral Samuel F. Dupont pulled out his surviving warships and wisely chose not to renew the attack.

With Charleston once again secure, rumors began flying that Beauregard would be ordered to part with a major portion of his command. Reinforcements would probably be dispatched to either Lee in Virginia or to the hard-pressed Pemberton at Vicksburg on the Mississippi River. Regardless of the destination, Gist was determined to be numbered with those departing.[38]

His decision was arrived at over time, his dissatisfaction stemming largely from the nature of siege warfare itself. Long periods of relative inactivity tried his patience. It had been a year of frustration — tied up at headquarters while battle raged at Secessionville, too late at Pocataligo, false alarms at Wilmington, a mere spectator in the repulse of the ironclads. Since donning Confederate gray General Gist had not led his men in so much as a skirmish.

Pride was involved too. As Adjutant and Inspector General of South Carolina Gist had been involved in the big picture, respected and obeyed as the senior military man in state service. Now his command had shrunk to a very limited piece of geography, however important strategically. It would be understandable to feel shackled and resentful. After all, at the opening gun of the war Brigadier General States Rights Gist was already at the pinnacle of the state's military hierarchy and Ripley, though a West Pointer, was a mere Lieutenant Colonel.

Gist's energetic and thorough attention to duty made him a valued subordinate. Beauregard could depend on him to get the job done, no doubt the reason he was given so many responsible assignments. But pre-war prominence in the discredited militia remained a stigma, most unaware of his efforts and successes at reform. Outside the circle of his closest associates, States Rights Gist was for the most part an easily remembered name and little more.[39]

He was ready for a change. It may have been at the review of the troops in late April that Gist made his wishes known. Beauregard came to James Island to present new battle flags to the regiments. After the ceremony was an ideal time for Gist to talk to his chief. Old Bory explained that he had already promised General Hagood command of the first brigade ordered west or north, but Gist was insistent; probably all the more so since he knew that "Shanks" Evans was returning again to shrink his command. According to the disappointed Hagood, "Gist claimed his seniority." When orders came he would lead the departing troops.[40]

Those troops accepted Beauregard's thirteen-star standards "with three cheers and a Tiger."[41] Patriotic enthusiasm flourished in the sunshine of the Confederacy's third spring. On May 2 the daring Lee, his Army of Northern Virginia outnumbered more than two-to-one, turned the Federal flank at Chancellorsville. It was a stunning victory against overwhelming odds and spurred renewed hope for similar Southern success in the West. If the drama was nearing its climax, Gist expected to be at center stage.

Chapter Eight
"Sanctify Yourselves Against To Morrow"

There would be no delay. Convinced Charleston was for the present out of danger, the War Department on May 2 ordered that Beauregard send upwards of 10,000 men to Pemberton's relief. The South Carolina commander pleaded that he had just returned two brigades to North Carolina and a further transfer of such magnitude would be suicidal. The most he could spare would be 5,000, one-third of his command. Richmond concurred, and urged their swift dispatch.[1]

Beauregard began assembling those reinforcements around Brigadier Generals Gist and William Henry Talbot Walker. Gist's brigade would be made up of the 46th Georgia Regiment (under his senior Colonel Peyton H. Colquitt), the 16th South Carolina (Colonel James McCullough), the 24th South Carolina (Colonel Clement Hoffman Stevens), the 8th Georgia Battalion (Captain Z.L. Watters) and Captain T.B. Ferguson's battery of field artillery. In a letter to Pemberton, Beauregard described the two brigades as "the best that could be spared, under two of my ablest generals" and expressed hope that his men would be returned by early fall. To strengthen that possibility he urged Pemberton to "keep these troops together, under the command of General Gist, in preference to putting them separately in other divisions." Beauregard offered to send Johnson Hagood to command one of the brigades if that would keep the little division intact under Gist.[2]

The logistics of the exodus were formidable. 5,000 soldiers with their arms and equipment were to be transported across Dixie from South Carolina and Georgia on the South's broken-down railroads. Gist arranged for his contingent to begin departing Charleston on May 6. Going first would be the 8th Georgia Battalion, the 24th South Carolina, and part of the 46th Georgia; all under the command of Colonel Colquitt. The remainder of the brigade would join the procession over the next two days, the General himself bringing up the rear. Walker would come up from Georgia.[3] With orders issued and preparations going forward under competent subordinates, Gist had one important item of personal business. He was getting married.

The hastily-arranged ceremony would have scandalized a previous generation. But so many conventions were being swept away by wartime necessity. There could be no round of parties, traditional wedding trip or elaborate bridal wardrobe. And so many family members and friends would be absent. It was too short notice to hope that Janie's older sister Mary could make her way from Edgefield, South Carolina. At least younger sisters Laura, Ellen and Caroline would brighten the occasion. And States could rely on brother James standing at his side.

Despite the circumstances, family and servants could be depended on to make Janie's wedding day happy and memorable. The roses were in full bloom for the May 6 Episcopal ceremony at Live Oak Plantation. "Bless O Lord, this ring," prayed the minister, "that he who gives it and she who wears it may abide in thy peace, and continue in thy favor, unto their life's end..." Parting was surely the most rending moment of their lives, the war's cruelest wound thus far. The couple would have no more than forty-eight hours together as man and wife before States again buckled on his sword and raced to catch up with the Mississippi-bound train.[4]

Those troop trains rattled along over worn-out rails at a top-speed seldom exceeding fifteen miles-per-hour. Dixie's railroads were a patchwork of shortlines handicapped by differing gauges of track, decrepit equipment and lackadaisical management. But what a spectacle it was! Every variety of passenger and freight car was pressed into service, as many as forty-five soldiers sprawled across each rough, wooden floor. Those two runs to Wilmington had been valuable experience after all. As the parade crept through South Carolina hundreds of local boys jumped off to make unauthorized visits home. Officers were left at Branchville and Augusta, Georgia to round them up. Stops were frequent. The journey was broken by tiresome changing of trains, and even two short hops by boat in Alabama.[5]

Everywhere crowds came out to show their patriotic devotion. "The ladies all along...give the men flowers, when we stop," wrote Colonel Capers, describing the triumphal review in letters to his wife. "Every house, station, village, or town we pass, the ladies, old and young, and the children, white and black, flock to wave their handkerchiefs and hands, and in some cases Confederate flags. Our men wave their hats and shout at the top of their voices." The good-natured boys were having the time of their lives. "Really, I have laughed a great deal this morning," confessed the Colonel as he recounted the antics of a trio of regimental clowns. "Clarence, who is all life and fun, and Holmes and Forest, went out on the platform and would shout 'good-bye' and halloo at the most amusing rate and it occurred so often, and the dear noble women seemed so much in earnest, that the 'good-bye' of Clarence and Forest seemed a farce." The "Marion Rifles Glee Club," from Company A of the 24th Regiment, performed at stops in return for the refreshments and hospitality.[6]

Gist was about two days behind the leading elements of his divided brigade. On the twelfth he telegraphed Pemberton from Montgomery, Alabama saying that he expected to arrive in Jackson on May 14, reiterating Beauregard's desire that the command be kept together. The first of the brigade leaped from the cars in the Mississippi capital the night of the thirteenth. General Joseph E. Johnston stepped to the platform from the same train after traveling a roundabout route from Tennessee.[7] Ordered to Mississippi to take charge of a deteriorating situation, Johnston would need every soldier now rushing to his aid.

For almost a year the Federal objective in the West had been Vicksburg on the Mississippi River. The previous summer the Yankee navy had managed to run the gauntlet of her batteries, but effective contol of the waterway would never belong to the Federals as long as Southern guns frowned from Vicksburg's bluffs. In December Major General Ulysses S. Grant failed in his first attempt to capture the city. Despairing of gaining the stronghold by direct assault, in late April Grant succeeded in landing his army on the eastern bank of the river south of Vicksburg and marched inland. To prevent his foes from concentrating against him, Grant hurried to position his men between Johnston and Pemberton. He would neutralize the Confederates at Jackson then turn his attention to Vicksburg, the real objective.

Complaining that he was too late to save the capital, within hours after arriving Johnston withdrew his troops northward. He called on the soldiers of Gist's and Walker's brigades to cover his retreat. Gist's understrength regiments, still under the temporary command of Colonel Colquitt, took up a position at Wright's farm with orders to hold the enemy until instructed to retire. In a driving rainstorm the vastly superior Northern force slammed into the South Carolinians. Colquitt's men succeeded in their mission of holding on for two long hours, losing nearly 200 men yet inflicting 300 casualties. The Unionists made their final charge only to discover that the Rebels had made good their escape.[8]

Unaware of the battle and evacuation of Jackson, Gist reached Brandon east of the capital on the afternoon of the fourteenth and there was warned to proceed with caution. Four miles farther down the line a dispatch arrived from Johnston ordering him to withdraw to some point forty or fifty miles distant. Gist obediently reversed engines and backed-up to Forest Station. There he established head-quarters, set up a telegraph, sent for supplies for his 1,500 men and asked Johnston for further instructions.[9]

Johnston directed Gist to join him at Calhoun Station, seven miles south of Canton. Again the brigade rode the rails to Brandon. Discovering that Grant had evacuated Jackson, Gist marched in and took possession of the sacked and van-dalized city. Gathering up Confederate brigades as he mov-ed forward, the South Carolinian finally linked up with Johnston between Canton and the capital.[10]

Gist had hurried to his General only to be assigned gar-rison duty. Johnston with his few men had no intention of plunging westward after Grant. During these days of relative inactivity, Gist had time to pen a lengthy letter to Beauregard, reporting on an eventful three weeks. The proud Brigadier could not resist mentioning that he had under his command six brigades, numbering 12,000 gray-clad veterans, at this moment a larger force than Beauregard himself command-ed.[11]

The previous day Gist had sent Brigadier General Walker on a mission across the Big Black River to secure strategic Yazoo City. Walker would not remain his subordinate for long. The distinguished Georgian was a United States Military Academy graduate of 1837 and wore scars from the Seminole and Mexican Wars. He resigned from the U.S. Ar-my the day South Carolina seceded and soon accepted a Con-federate brigadier general's stars. In late April 1861 he resigned his commission, ostensibly for reasons of ill health, and accepted a major general's commission from the state of Georgia. In early 1863 he re-entered Confederate service as a brigadier general. Thus, young Gist outranked the old warrior until Walker's long-expected promotion to major general came in late May. Walker's new division was the very force that Gist had proudly, if briefly, headed. Gist resumed command of his South Carolinians and Georgians; the brigade that now bore his name still part of Walker's division, Army of the Department of Mississippi and Eastern Louisiana.[12]

While Johnston marshaled his forces, Pemberton made a forlorn effort to unite the two armies. As he sallied forth from Vicksburg he was careful to leave the river city well-guarded. Halfway between Vicksburg and Jackson, Grant intercepted and gave battle at Champion's Hill, soundly defeating the Rebels. Whipped and demoralized, Pemberton's men just managed to slip back into Vicksburg's well-prepared defenses. Sensing victory, Grant ordered an all-out assault. But once behind earthworks and cotton bales the Southerners regained their resolve. The attacking Federals lost 3,200 men in a storm of Confederate fire. Grant then laid siege to the city. With 70,000 soldiers at his disposal, he simultaneously threw up defenses in his rear to insure against interference from Johnston.

Johnston was not about to interfere. Secretary of War James A. Seddon, speaking for the Confederate President, bombarded the General with telegrams urging action. Realizing that Vicksburg's loss would split the country, Johnston was prodded to attack at all costs. But risking his men and reputation in a daring gamble was simply not Johnston's style. In his mind Vicksburg itself was lost anyway. He wished that Pemberton could somehow struggle free and save the city's defenders, yet Johnston had no real plan to come to his aid. He seemed not to comprehend Pemberton's helplessness and desperation. Through June, Johnston kept his army of 28,000 hovering in Grant's rear, safely out of action; finally on June 29 beginning an extensive reconnaissance of Federal positions along the Big Black. In the middle of his cautious inspection, the starving Vicksburg garrison surrendered.

Grant could now concentrate on his eastern front, unleashing in that direction a strong force commanded by

Major General William Tecumseh Sherman. After a week of intense fighting, Johnston was forced to evacuate Jackson once again and retreat eastward on the night of July 16. Sherman lingered for a time, burning and looting, then returned to Vicksburg — devastating the countryside as he went. "Sherman's sentinels" marked the way: blackened chimneys guarding sites where homes once stood.

It had been only two months since Gist and his men rode into the Magnolia State light-hearted and confident of saving Pemberton. Now the Capital City was in ruins and Vicksburg engulfed by the blue tide. Colonel Capers summarized the grueling and discouraging campaign: "The marches and counter-marches to which they were subjected in the heat of summer, the men for the most of the time badly supplied with shoes and actually, at times, suffering for water fit to drink, fully tested the spirit and discipline of the brigade."[13]

Impure water led to an outbreak of typhoid while the brigade camped at Morton, Mississippi. Dr. Thomas L. Ogier, division surgeon, contracted the disease and died. Also stricken was James Gist. The young officer was carried to the home of a Dr. Whitehead in Morton and there given the best care available. At first he seemed to improve, then rapidly grew worse. As he lay dying he asked friends to read to him from the Bible; his feverish mind wandering back to boyhood days with his family at Wyoming. His death on August 24 deeply affected fellow officers. The thirty-year-old was well-liked and much admired as a kind man, "always ready for any duty."[14]

From Gettysburg to Vicksburg it had been a summer of disaster for the Confederate cause; for Gist himself a season of personal tragedy. Still grieving for his brother, the General and his men in late August received word that they were to be reassigned. There would be no return to the Palmetto State. General Braxton Bragg's army in Chattanooga desperately needed help. The Union Army of the Cumberland was advancing relentlessly across the mountains of eastern Tennessee, in the words of Lincoln's War Secretary, "to give the finishing blow to the rebellion." The Yankee commander, Major General William S. Rosecrans, probably believed his adversaries were in demoralized flight as the Southerners abandoned Chattanooga and fell back into northern Georgia. But these Rebels were not through. By rail from Mississippi came the divisions of Walker and John C. Breckinridge. In secrecy, Lee was preparing to detach Lieutenant General James Longstreet's corps of 15,000 from the Army of Northern Virginia and in a logistical miracle shift this force to Bragg. The Confederate Army of Tennessee would be ready for the coming test.

Bragg posted Gist's brigade for the time being on his extreme left at Rome, Georgia in support of the cavalry on that flank.[15]

In Rome on that second Sunday in September a somber and pensive General Gist accompanied Colonel Capers to church services. The sermon was from chapter seven, verse thirteen of the Old Testament book of Joshua. It seemed to hold answers for the discerning. Like ancient Israel, the Southern people had suffered hard blows, though engaged in a righteous cause. Surely there was in defeat a higher purpose at work, a warning from the Almighty to put away selfish disobedience.[16] "Sanctify yourselves against to morrow..." commanded the Lord of Hosts. There was hope in the challenge.

Chapter Nine
"Gist's Brigade is Just Coming Up"

Winding through the mountain passes, Rosecrans' divided army seemed an inviting target. With bold leadership and a little luck, Bragg might actually destroy his adversary's columns one at a time. This was his fond expectation when on September 9 he directed Major General Thomas Carmichael Hindman and Lieutenant General Daniel Harvey Hill to attack one advanced Union division. But on the morning set for battle Hindman delayed and Hill made excuses while the Federals slipped out of reach. Two days later Bragg sent Lieutenant General Leonidas Polk after Yankees similarly exposed at Lee and Gordon's Mill on the Chickamauga River. While the cautious Polk slowly maneuvered into position, his mind dwelt on all that could go wrong. Pleading that the odds had turned against him, he canceled the attack. Bragg was furious. He faulted his subordinates for failure to carry out his plan while they pointed to what they considered indecisive orders and inept leadership for the lost opportunities. Sadly, there was truth in both charges.

Eleven years older than Bragg, Polk, like his commander, was a North Carolinian and West Point educated.

Soon after graduation Polk resigned his commission to enter the ministry, and over the years he rose in the Episcopal Church to the office of bishop. When war came he unhesitatingly took up the sword, proclaiming, "We of the Confederate States are the last bulwarks of civil and religious liberty..." Polk designed for his men a variation of the Southern battle flag that was inspired by his denomination's cross of Saint George. An old friend of President Davis, some would argue that promotion came too quickly to the Bishop-General.[1] Bragg's military career included combat in Mexico where his ability and bravery did not go unnoticed by fellow soldier Jefferson Davis. Known as a stickler for red tape and regulations, Bragg was far abler an organizer than he was a field commander of a great army. Yet even his severest critics never questioned his fiery devotion to the Southern cause. Now at the pinnacle of his career, poor health weakened and made him irritable.

With his early opportunities gone, the most cheering sound to Bragg's ear was the scream of the locomotive whistle. Those long-expected reinforcements from Virginia arrived on each train, and his own scattered forces were gathering in. With 71,500 troops under his command, Bragg would soon enjoy that rarest of Confederate advantages: numerical superiority. Still determined to seize the initiative, he began throwing divisions across Chickamauga Creek to confront the now concentrated Army of the Cumberland.

Down in Rome, Gist received Bragg's order on the afternoon of Thursday, September 17 to report with his brigade to Ringgold. Next morning trains arrived, according to plan, but with too few cars. Gist departed with the 24th South Carolina, the 8th Georgia battalion, three companies of the 46th Georgia and Ferguson's battery. The 16th South Carolina and the greater part of the 46th Georgia would have to follow later. The journey went well until the brigade rolled into Kingston. There they were shunted onto a siding where Gist could only watch as the slow-moving trains up from Atlanta passed with those cocky Eastern troops on their way to reinforce Bragg.

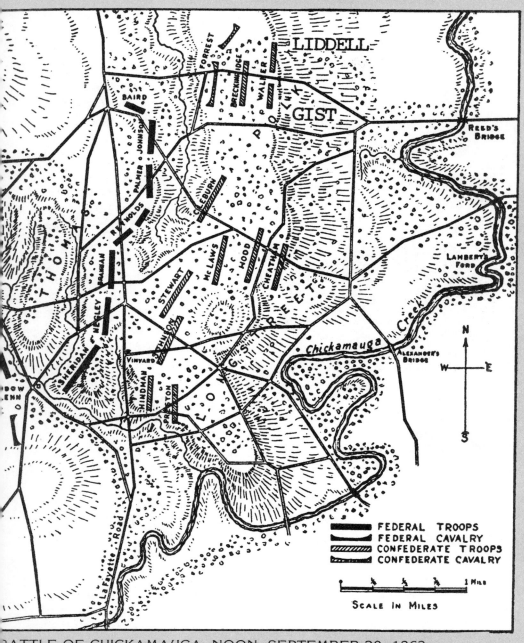

BATTLE OF CHICKAMAUGA, NOON, SEPTEMBER 20, 1863

(Reprinted from James Longstreet: Lee's War Horse by H. J. Eckenrode and Bryan Conrad. © 1936, 1986 The University of North Carolina Press. Used by permission of the publisher.)

Clement H. Stevens, commander
of the 24th South Carolina
Regiment. General Gist
commended him for
"distinguished gallantry" at
Chickamauga.
(South Caroliniana Library)

Chafing at the delay, yet trying to be patient, Gist found the transportation agent and secured that official's solemn promise that additional cars would be promptly sent to Rome for the rest of the men. Longstreet's corps had passed by dark, and Gist expected his brigade to be next. But impatience turned to anger on checking the cab: The engine driver and crew had abandoned the locomotive and extinguished the fire! Colonels Colquitt, Stevens and Capers spread out in search of the faithless engineer and found him sleeping soundly. His mumbled excuses about trouble with the machinery failed to convince his captors. Finally he admitted to simple exhaustion. "Colonel Stevens drew his pistol," recounted Capers, "but that did not move him, and then he told him that he would put a man on the engine to run it, and men to fire it, and when it was ready if he did not come and take charge he would kill him."[2]

Thanks to the eloquent Stevens, Gist's brigade was on its way again. Somehow the somnolent supervisor and amateur crew kept the train on the tracks until they reached the end of the line next morning. There at Catoosa wood station the men detrained while Gist rode on ahead to Ringgold where he could telegraph Bragg for further instructions. While awaiting his commanding general's reply, Gist again wired the agent of the Western and Atlantic Railroad in Kingston to hurry-on those men still waiting down in Rome.

He also tried to round-up wagons for the supply of ammunition he had brought along. Finally, Bragg ordered Gist to wait for a large ammunition train that was being formed, then guard and convey that wagon train to army field headquarters. As the day wore on Gist prepared his men for the march and found a knowledgeable guide by the name of Dr. Evans.

He would need someone to show him the way to Chickamauga Creek, especially as darkness was coming. It was almost ten that night before the officer in charge of the ammunition train reported to Gist and the convoy set out. The brigade groped through the darkness, slowed by the wagons, but reached Alexander's Bridge at daybreak of the twentieth. Gist immediately reported to headquarters and was relieved to shed himself of responsibility for the train. There his 980 exhausted men dropped to the ground to steal a few minutes of precious sleep while their General waited on superiors to decide what to do with them.[3]

The battle's climactic second day began not at all as Bragg had planned. The previous day's engagement had been indecisive and haphazard as both armies struggled back-and-forth for supremacy along a three-mile front, much of the land covered with dense woods. Darkness brought an end to the fighting, but throughout the night Rosecrans' army dug-in and prepared for the attack they knew was coming. Bragg ordered a dawn assault, but confusion and misunderstanding delayed the advance. Finally at 9:30 a.m. Daniel Harvey Hill, on the Confederate right, sent forward two divisions under Major Generals John C. Breckinridge and Patrick R. Cleburne. The Yankees were by then well-prepared and the attack was soon in trouble. Confederate Brigadier General Benjamin Hardin Helm's brigade was repulsed with severe losses and their gallant commander mortally wounded.

The Federals made no immediate move to follow-up on their advantage, but Hill began casting about for men to fill the breach. Hearing of the arrival of Gist's brigade, he sent a staff officer to Major General Walker, commander of the reserve corps, requesting Gist's help in restoring the line. Somehow the order was garbled and Walker advanced his entire corps of two divisions to Hill's assistance, accompanied by Polk, commander of the right wing. Gist rode up at the moment the other three generals met. Quickly Walker placed the South Carolinian in command of a division made up of his own, Matthew Ector's and Claudius Wilson's brigades. As Gist was turning away to take charge of his division, Hill again asked Walker for a brigade to support Breckinridge. Walker suggested the nearest, one from Brigadier General St. John R. Liddell's command. Hill was insistent: He had heard of Gist's brigade and they were the men he wanted.

"Gist's brigade is just coming up," replied Walker. Hill instructed Colonel Colquitt, commanding Gist's brigade as senior officer, to advance in support of Breckinridge's troops. Hill ordered Gist himself to stand in readiness with Ector's and Wilson's brigades. Colonel Colquitt and his men entered the woods and ran into a strong force of the enemy secure behind breastworks of fallen trees. The Confederates he was ordered to support simply were not there. The brigade was devastated by enemy bullets but under the steadfast leadership of Colquitt, Stevens, and Capers stood its ground and returned fire. For at least twenty-five minutes the killing went on. Colquitt fell mortally wounded; Stevens and Capers were seriously hurt. One-third of the brigade was either killed or injured, including all but two of its field officers. Finally Hill permitted Gist to advance the remainder of his division, arriving in time to cover the withdrawal of the decimated brigade. The Lieutenant General ordered the line re-formed near the position held prior to the attack.[4]

Bragg's ill-prepared and badly-executed assault on the right had failed to dislodge the enemy, but the effort had succeeded in weakening the Union forces facing Longstreet on the left. All day a steady stream of reinforcements poured to Rosecrans' threatened flank. In this fluid and confused situation, a Federal staff officer made what he perceived to be a startling discovery: There seemed to be a fatal gap in the line facing Longstreet. Rosecrans immediately ordered Brigadier General Thomas J. Wood, commanding a division, to fill the hole by shifting to the left.

The imagined breach did not exist. The young staff officer had failed to see his own troops hidden by the trees. Wood himself was bewildered. He knew the order was filled with danger, but only an hour before Rosecrans had verbally blistered the Brigadier for not following specific directions. His ears still burning from the rebuke, Wood was in no mood to question orders or use his own discretion. Obediently he marched his men out of line, creating an opening where none had existed.

Longstreet knew nothing of the blunder, but was at that moment preparing to attack. Within minutes, five Rebel divisions charged into the gap and quickly made the most of their good luck. Torn asunder, the Yankee right began falling back in disorder while Rosecrans and much of his army fled the field. Major General George H. Thomas stubbornly delayed the Southern onslaught on Snodgrass Hill throughout the afternoon. His gallant resistance to repeated assaults saved Rosecrans' army from destruction and would earn Thomas the sobriquet "Rock of Chickamauga."

As Longstreet rolled forward, the divisions of Liddell and Gist remained inactive on the extreme right of Polk's wing. They were now favorably positioned to strike the flank and rear of the defeated Federals. But instead of attempting to coordinate such a movement, Polk was satisfied to order a general advance of his entire wing about 4 p.m.

Fearing that the Federal left would indeed be cut off and destroyed, Thomas ordered one final and desperate attack against those advancing Rebels who threatened his withdrawal. For the task he chose Brigadier General John Turchin's brigade of Ohioans and Kentuckians. Though he now called Illinois home, Turchin shouted orders in the heaviest of Russian accents. Born a subject of the Tsar, and trained in the Imperial Guard, Ivan Vasilovich Turchinoff was now entrusted with ensuring the escape of the endangered divisions. Turchin's bluecoats surprised Liddell's division on the Chattanooga Road and threw them back under heavy fire.[5]

Gist's division now came at Turchin alone: his own brigade on the right, Wilson's in the center and Ector's on the left. Gist had been reinforced by the tardy arrival from Rome of seven companies of the 46th Georgia, and now through the woods and into the blue ranks they charged; the Georgians furious to avenge the fallen Colquitt. Gist's powerful counterattack sent the Yankee force reeling, but it was too late to pursue. By now darkness was falling and Turchin had accomplished his objective of buying time for the Union withdrawal. There was nothing left for Gist to do but establish a defensive line, tend to the dead and wounded, and send prisoners to the rear. "The firing ceased," reported Gist, "loud cheers went up to heaven, and the grandest, most important battle of the war was fought and won."[6]

Grand perhaps. But it had been one of the bloodiest days in American history. Losses on both sides were staggering. Gist's understrength brigade alone suffered 336 dead, wounded and missing. The day after the battle, Gist reported an aggregate strength of only 1,913 for the entire division.[7] Bragg counted 20,950 casualties while inflicting a loss of 16,179 on the enemy. Among the wounded was Lieutenant Colonel Joseph Fincher Gist of the 15th South Carolina, the General's oldest brother.[8] Perhaps it was the magnitude of his losses, or simply lack of imagination and poor generalship as his critics charged, but Bragg failed to chase his beaten adversaries. Rosecrans' army fell back into Chattanooga largely unmolested as the Confederate victors slowly took up positions on heights surrounding the city. The siege was on.

"I witnessed nothing but a heroism that was worthy of men battling for their freedom," wrote General Walker after Chickamauga. His two subordinates, Gist and Liddell, came in for high praise. "I have only to say that the brigadier-generals fought with a gallantry that entitles them to division commands..." Remembering the battle, one of Gist's company commanders wrote of "the cool determined courage of Genl. Gist, whose bearing particularly struck me. I saw and spoke with him in the morning and again in the afternoon, he followed close up with our lines, and stood, in contrast with many others in high rank, with self-possessed coolness and efficiency, from the first to the last."[9]

Bragg had won his victory and now had his former pursuers pinned-down in Chattanooga. Their backs to the Tennessee River, the Federals were cut off by Confederates on Lookout Mountain to the west and Missionary Ridge to the south and east. Except for one round-about wagon road, all traffic into the city was at the mercy of Southern guns. But Lincoln had no intention of letting go. Federals from as far away as Maryland began a long journey to reinforce the besieged city.

By mid-October Rosecrans was replaced by Thomas, with Grant in overall command. On the Confederate side too there was a shake-up in leadership, with Bragg seemingly more interested in settling scores with subordinates than in taking Chattanooga. He arrested Polk for slowness in attacking on the twentieth. Other generals were stung by Bragg's wrath or shocked by his failure to follow-up the Chickamauga victory. Army morale suffered. A petition to President Davis in October, signed by four corps commanders and eight other generals, asked that Bragg be replaced. The situation seemed serious enough for Davis to visit his Western army in person. The President called a joint meeting of Bragg and his critics, and probably hoping to foster unity and encourage a show of support for the army commander, asked each officer's opinion of the man. In a scene that must have been as embarrassing to his subordinates as it was humiliating to Bragg, Davis was shocked by the frank denunciations that he heard. Disappointed by the depth of the senior generals' opposition, Davis yet felt that he had no choice but to support Bragg. How could a general be removed less than three weeks after his greatest victory? To relieve the friction,

Bragg's most open and vocal critics would themselves be reassigned.

If the chief executive seemed blind to Bragg's shortcomings, Davis was himself a victim of mean-spirited criticism and backbiting that hurt the Southern cause and would have destroyed a lesser man. Religiously observing his brother's feud with the President, Armand Beauregard asked Gist to order him away so as to avoid any contact with Davis during the visit. In a letter to the Charleston commander, brother Armand relished every detail of his intended snub.[10]

The Beauregard family's fuming was only Gist's latest opportunity to polish his diplomatic skills. From his early exposure to the Byzantine politics of antebellum South Carolina, to Governor Pickens' dispute with militiaman Simons, and now in Bragg's clash with his lieutenants; Gist possessed a knack for remaining on good terms with all parties. Perhaps what seemed an ingratiating trait was in fact a fixed determination to shun the petty self-seeking he saw around him. Gist surely had his opinions, but there is no evidence the young General was anything but a peacemaker. Davis made a statement to the soldiers during his inspection that Gist would have seconded unreservedly. "When the war shall have ended," reminded the commmander-in-chief, "the highest meed of praise will be due to him who has claimed the less for himself in proportion to the service he has rendered."[11]

In the subsequent reorganization Hill and Polk were out of the picture. Bragg divided his force into three corps under Longstreet, Breckinridge and Lieutenant General William J. Hardee.

The dispatch of Longstreet's corps on an ill-advised expedition towards Knoxville in early November reduced Bragg's long line confronting Chattanooga to 40,000. Inside the city, Grant's three armies under Sherman, Thomas and Major General Joseph Hooker had by now swollen to 60,000. It was time to plan a breakout. Grant proposed that Sherman with his four-division Army of the Tennessee hit the north end of Missionary Ridge. Linking up with Thomas' Army of the Cumberland, the Confederate flank could be rolled up and the Rebels driven southward off the high ground without resorting to an impossible frontal assault. Hooker's division from the Army of the Potomac would act as a reserve and hold at bay the Southern force occupying Lookout Mountain.

By the final week in November all seemed in readiness. The hill called Orchard Knob, a Rebel salient about a mile in front of Missionary Ridge, was taken with little difficulty the afternoon of the twenty-third. Now it was Sherman's turn. In darkness he quietly crossed the Tennessee River, secured a bridgehead, and by late afternoon of the twenty-fourth had his entire army ready to attack. But the surprise was on him. He seized the end of Missionary Ridge only to discover that a formidable ravine separated him from Confederate positions on Tunnel Hill to the south.

While Sherman was puzzling over his next move, down at Lookout Mountain the Confederate army was paralyzed by indecision. Bragg seemed unsure of his troop dispositions or even whether to hold the mountain. Through most of the siege Walker's division, still temporarily under Gist's command, had been posted on a line west of the Chattanooga Creek to the base of Lookout Mountain.[12] On the sixteenth, Gist was ordered with two of his brigades to climb the heights and reinforce the command there.[13]

From an artillery position near the peak Colonel James C. Nisbet of Gist's command whiled away the time enjoying the scenery while daring Federal sharpshooters. The Colonel would deliberately make himself a tempting target to the riflemen far down in the valley. When he observed a puff of smoke he would slip behind cover and wait for the whine of the bullet. Then he sportingly repeated the performance with the comment that the disappointed marksman "deserved another chance."[14]

Nisbet's game ended on the twenty-third. Anticipating an attack on his other flank, Bragg withdrew Gist and his men and sent them to Cleburne holding the extreme right on Missionary Ridge. "The withdrawal of Walker's division, on the night of the 23d," concluded the Confederate commander on Lookout Mountain, Major General Carter L. Stevenson, "in my opinion, rendered the position on the left, opposed by so large a force, untenable..."[15] The day after Gist's redeployment the Federals attacked with a four-to-one numerical advantage. Much of the time the fighting was obscured by a thick fog that would later inspire the exalted name Battle Above the Clouds for the relatively minor engagement. On the night of the twenty-fourth Stevenson abandoned his position and fell back to Missionary Ridge.

Both defender and attacker knew that while the flanks might possibly be turned, there on the ridge the Confederate army was invulnerable to frontal assault. The assumption that those defenses would never be tested led to carelessness. Artillery was casually posted at the summit; an imposing position to be sure, but not practical for sweeping an assaulting force. At the base of the ridge rifle pits were dug. In the event of an attack the men there were under orders to fire a volley then scramble up the heights to the main line at the crest. Under Bragg's orders that line had itself become dangerously thin, as he expected the real threat to come on his right at Tunnel Hill where Sherman remained poised to attack Cleburne.

Born in Ireland, Patrick Ronayne Cleburne received his first military training in Her Majesty's 41st Regiment of Foot before immigrating to America at age twenty-one. Arkansas became his adopted home and states' rights his creed. Promotion in the Southern Provisional Army came quickly to this brilliant fighter. Characteristically, Cleburne carefully prepared his defenses.

Like Cleburne, Gist personally saw to the posting of his artillery. Finding that the horses could not do the job, an infantry company was assigned to each gun with responsibility for cutting a road where necessary and hauling it up the ridge. General Gist made sure that all of the twelve-pounders could fire over the heads of his infantrymen from the heights to the rear. To Gist's right, on the other side of the railroad tunnel, was Stevenson's division. Cleburne's men held the extreme flank. Gist's infantry line was too thin to inspire much confidence, but the terrain here was particularly steep.[16]

Sherman hit Cleburne at dawn of the twenty-fifth. From well-prepared positions, and under able leadership, the Confederates beat off one Union attack after another. Federals briefly established a precarious foothold on Tunnel Hill only to be thrown back by a furious Rebel charge. Hundreds of Yankees were captured along with eight of their battle flags. George Earl Maney's brigade of Gist's division flew to Cleburnes's support and fought magnificently, taking part in the charge and bringing back a stand of captured colors.[17]

Gist and the rest of his command on Cleburne's left had similar success but an easier time of it. When at first light the enemy approached Gist's front Colonel Nisbet, without instructions, rode up to Lieutenant René Toutant Beauregard's battery and ordered him to open fire. "Have you an order to that effect?" asked the jumpy artilleryman, son of General Beauregard. "Commence firing lieutenant," replied Nisbet, "What we see is order enough for me." Beauregard's six Napoleans cut loose and were instantly joined by Captain Evan Howell's battery. The combination of canister and forbidding terrain kept the advance from becoming more than a demonstration. The Union soldiers halted in front of the ridge, many seeking shelter in the tunnel itself. During a lull, part of the 39th Georgia of Stevenson's command charged down the ridge and took prisoners before being ordered back. Again the Federals came against the ridge and again cannon fire alone was enough to stay them. Gist was trying to get a closer look at the action when a Yankee bullet brought down his horse. The unfortunate General turned to nearby Captain John Steinmeyer to complain that Chickamauga had cost him one horse and now the enemy had killed another.[18]

From his headquarters on Orchard Knob, Grant surveyed the panorama of battle. Hooker had been delayed, but by afternoon was at least threatening the Confederate left. Sherman was getting nowhere. To relieve the pressure on Sherman, and at the same time assist Hooker, Grant late in the day ordered Thomas to make a demonstration against the Confederate center on Missionary Ridge. It was an awesome spectacle as four divisions stepped forward. As ordered, the Confederates at the base of the ridge fired, then turned around and began the upward climb. Not all though. Inexplicably, some in the rifle pits never got word they were to withdraw and heroically held their ground until overwhelmed. Capturing the base of the ridge, the Federals had orders to halt until Grant decided what to do with them. Massed there, tormented by fire from above and encouraged by their apparent success, determination swept from one end of the blue line to the other. Horrified and helpless, Grant watched his now out-of-control troops scaling the heights, perhaps to their destruction.

But the defects in Bragg's defensive plan were fast becoming obvious. Defenders on the crest discovered that they were unable to fire downward without exposing themselves. Much of the time they hesitated for fear of hitting their own men retreating from those abandoned rifle pits. Many on the crest were never told to expect the withdrawal of the forward line, making it appear to them that defeat was under way. To this combination was added the most volatile ingredient of all: the spirit of the attackers. They seemed possessed by an exultant if suicidal passion to have their victory. No longer were they individuals struggling up a mountainside. They melted into an irresistible blue wave. In quick succession, Grant saw the regimental banners of the Army of the Cumberland breaking out on the ridge.

Bragg in person vainly attempted to shore up his disintegrating center. The men yelled with derision at their commander's appeals to rally around him. "Boys, get away the best you can!" shouted the more realistic Breckinridge.[19]

Miles to the right Gist and Cleburne, from their separate vantage points, were congratulating themselves on a splendid victory. It was nearly twilight now and Sherman was no nearer his objective of turning the flank than he had been at daybreak. Then Cleburne received disturbing word that Hardee needed reinforcements, and he set out with them himself. About the same time, with his front quiet again, Gist also left his division. He too may have heard of the trouble at the center. Neither general could have guessed that their work for the day was only beginning.[20]

Learning of the disaster, Cleburne was ordered by Hardee to form a new line at right angle across the ridge to protect the flank until the men could be withdrawn. While Confederates in the center were in full flight down the rear of the mountain, the victorious Southerners of Gist's command were lighting campfires and preparing supper when Cleburne and his staff galloped up with news of the defeat. Asking for Gist, Cleburne ordered the cumbersome artillery to begin pulling out immediately. After some delay the generals found each other and Cleburne ordered Gist to form his division across the ridge, a movement that despite the confusion was probably already underway. Union forces that turned to attack in Gist's direction were, in General Thomas' words, "obstinately resisted," making little progress until darkness extinguished their fire.[21]

Lieutenant Beauregard fretted over his artillery pieces. Getting them down the ridge seemed impossible in the darkness with only poor roads and half-dead horses. "In fact," recalled Nisbet, "he was so troubled the tears came in his eyes."

"I will stand by you," reassured the Colonel. "I have some men hunting for torch pine. We will have torches soon. I will keep my own regiment with your battery."

The torch bearers reported finding a "sorter-of-a-little, old, blind wood road" down the ridge to the rear. Locking the wheels of the gun carriages with rope and chain, the guns were eased down the slope in a freezing rain. With his precious Napoleans again on level ground Beauregard could breathe a little easier.

"Now we are all right, if the Yanks don't advance and capture the whole shooting match," concluded Nisbet.[22]

Gist's division was to serve as rearguard for Breckinridge's corps, while Cleburne protected Hardee's retreat. As it turned out, Maney's brigade of Gist's division assisted Hardee next day in attacking and driving back Federal pursuers. Nisbet's and Maney's men struggled to get across a stream and on the road to Ringgold.

"Just as my last wagon was passing around the hill," recounted Nisbet, "I saw Maney draw up his Tennesseans in line to receive a brigade of blue-coats who were advancing in line of battle across the opposite field. General Maney had just got his last cannon over the branch and on the road. He waited until the Yank's line was broken in crossing the branch. Then he charged, driving them back. But Maney was brought to my camp at Ringgold that night severely wounded."[23]

Gist's men finally reached Ringgold and rested there. "But the enemy was pressing in on us with large bodies of infantry," remembered Nisbet. "It was decided that the victorious army had to be checked or we would lose our wagons and artillery. The demoralized divisions were allowed to pass on in retreat."[24]

General Hooker's 16,000 Federals were in hot pursuit and to save the army Bragg called on Cleburne. The Irishman set a trap, carefully placing his 4,000 men and artillery in a narrow gorge in Taylor's Ridge where the Western and Atlantic Railroad passed through. There they hid and waited. When Union troops were within fifty yards he opened a devastating fire. For five hours Cleburne's Confederates beat off repeated assaults while Walker's division under Gist waited unneeded in reserve behind the ridge. Finally, Hooker disengaged. With Cleburne's mission of delaying the enemy accomplished, Hardee ordered the rearguard to fall back as the army regrouped at Dalton, Georgia. For his brilliant

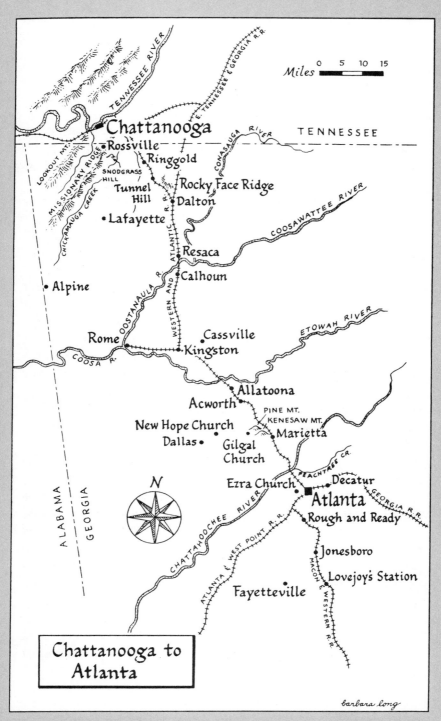

THE ATLANTA CAMPAIGN

(Reprinted from Their Tattered Flags; The Epic of the Confederacy by Frank E. Vandiver. Used by permission of Texas A & M University Press.)

action at Ringgold Gap, Cleburne received the official congratulations of the Confederate Congress.[25]

Days after the battle, Walker described how his division,
under Gist's command, had been forced to withdraw from
the ridge only after the Confederate left and center had given
way. "My division...behaved handsomely under its gallant
leader Genl. Gist. I am perfectly satisfied with its performance."[26]

At Gettysburg Lee had taken all the blame for failure
on himself. In the Chattanooga debacle Bragg began immediately to cast about for a scapegoat. He charged that
throughout the battle and afterwards Breckinridge was drunk
and unfit for duty. Writing twenty years later, Bragg went
so far as to claim that, "I sent for the commander of the Rear
Guard, Brig. Genl. Gist, of S.C., and told him not to leave
Genl. B[reckinridge] — and if necessary, to put him in a
wagon and haul him off. But under no circumstances to allow
him to give an order." Breckinridge's biographer makes a
convincing case that Bragg's accusations against the former
United States Vice President were overdrawn if not fabricated.
There is no corroborating evidence to support Bragg's story
that Gist received such instructions or that he attempted to
carry them out.[27]

"The enemy made pursuit as far as Ringgold," reported
Bragg officially, "but was so handsomely checked by Major
General Cleburne and Brigadier General Gist, in command
of their respective divisions, that he gave us but little an-
noyance." One of but a handful receiving their chief's com-
mendation, Bragg praised Gist as "distinguished for coolness,
gallantry and successful conduct throughout the
engagements and in the rear guard on the retreat."[28] If Bragg
blamed others for his blunders, he at least had the good grace
to credit those troops and commanders who kept his defeat
from becoming annihilation.

Chapter Ten
"The Finest One in This Army"

Braxton Bragg and his beaten and demoralized army were back where they had been at the end of summer. Within days Bragg resigned, handing over the ruins of his command temporarily to Hardee. When Hardee declined permanent responsibility, President Davis reluctantly tapped Joe Johnston. It was an agonizing decision. Davis and most of his cabinet had profound misgivings about Johnston's strategic sense and even questioned the General's willingness to fight. But the men in the army loved him and were delighted to learn of his appointment. Old Joe saw to it that their needs were met, never wasted lives in battle and inspired all with his soldierly appearance and supreme confidence. Deserters returned and morale rebounded with the increased rations, back pay and a liberal furlough policy.

Gist was back in command of his brigade since General Walker's return to divisional command. Walker had been promising Gist some leave time, and by December 11 the young General was ready to hold him to his promise. Bearing letters and accompanied by staff officers as anxious as he was to spend Christmas with family, he was soon on his way to South Carolina and Janie. Walker and others would be visited that winter and spring by their families, and Gist too looked forward to returning to Dalton with his young bride. It would not be a long furlough for there was much work to be done.

In rebuilding, Gist's brigade set the standard. Through the unusually hard winter there was drill, reviews, training sessions for junior officers, recreation and well-attended revival meetings. Gist and his men had gone into winter quarters on the Spring Place Road, two miles east of Dalton. "Their camp is a beautiful one," wrote an observer, "very nice, snug houses — wide streets regularly laid off and looking like a village — the men well clothed and shod — in excellent discipline and well drilled." Johnston complimented Gist and was reported to have said that the troops "look as if they had a man at their head who knew how to do his duty and who took an interest in his men." The press were upbeat in their comments too. "The men [of Gist's brigade] are in good health and excellent spirits, and feel confident of success," wrote a Charleston reporter. "General Gist has built a brigade chapel," he continued, "and himself and staff attend religious services, while all the colonels are deeply interested, and encourage religious services in their several regiments." A few weeks later a newspaperman from Columbia noted widespread revivals in the army, "and even now there is a most remarkable one in progress in Gist's Brigade." Before the opening of the spring campaign Colonel Capers could boast that "Gist's brigade is in fine condition for the work before it."[1]

During the winter at Dalton, Gist routinely took command of the division in Walker's absence. Anticipating Gist's promotion to major general, other officers began casting covetous eyes on his brigade of South Carolinians and Georgians. "I think from all indications that my friend General Gist must be promoted before long and if that should take place," confided newly-promoted Brigadier General Clement H. Stevens, "I am particularly anxious to have his brigade. It is not only the finest one in this army, but it is one of the best disciplined."[2]

For Gist to advance beyond the rank of brigadier general would be to overcome President Davis' longstanding policy of reserving higher rank for professionally-trained soldiers. This was not an insurmountable obstacle. The President's rule could be set aside for exceptional officers who by aptitude and industry had proven themselves worthy.[3] Gist during nine months in the West had built this kind of solid reputation with his superiors. More than competent, he could always be counted on to perform the task assigned him. Fresh in everyone's memory was his shining record at Chickamauga and Chattanooga, in each battle holding divisional command.

In February Major General Patton Anderson was ordered to Florida, creating a vacancy in Breckinridge's old division. On the twenty-third Johnston telegraphed President Davis with a request for Gist's promotion: "Brigadier-General Gist I earnestly recommend for the major-generalcy. He is the best qualified for the place, in my judgement." Johnston emphasized to the President how badly he needed "good major generals." The President's reply must have surprised Johnston as much as it disappointed Gist. "Before the receipt of your telegram of the 23d," said Davis, "Brigadier-General Bate had been promoted to succeed Major-General Anderson. I hope this will meet your want in that regard and be acceptable." Davis sent Bate's nomination to the Senate in May, where the promotion was approved to date from February 23.[4] William B. Bate was a Mexican War veteran and had performed admirably in Confederate service. In Davis' mind the most important consideration may have been that both Anderson and Bate were Tennesseans. The defeats of 1863 left their state overrun by the invading army. Tennessee's Governor Isham G. Harris was "in exile," serving on the staff of General Johnston until the Confederacy could liberate his homeland. In these circumstances President Davis was intent on maintaining Volunteer State representation among the generals of the Army of Tennessee.[5]

Major General William Henry Talbot Walker.
(Library of Congress)

Deep concern for his country's manpower shortage led General Cleburne to come forward with a bold plan that winter in Dalton. He proposed to enlist blacks in the Southern army (though many already served unofficially in non-combatant positions) and "guarantee freedom within a reasonable time to every slave in the South who shall remain true to the Confederacy in this war." On the night of January 2 he made his presentation to a meeting of corps and division commanders at Johnston's headquarters. Many officers serving under Cleburne supported their chief, but most of the generals, led by Walker, were adamantly opposed. By the end of the year the Confederacy would belatedly adopt a similar measure, but at this point the country was not ready for Cleburne's proposal. Because of its potentially divisive nature, President Davis ordered the matter dropped.

Walker was a troubled man as he lashed out against Cleburne. Frustrated by failure to win promotion, irritated by friction with other officers and distressed over a daughter's romantic entanglements, he was in no mood to restrain his anger or bridle his tongue. Gist was probably still in South Carolina when the controversy broke and took little or no part in the debate, though there is evidence he sided with his friend Walker.[6]

Despite a long winter of reorganization and renewal, Johnston could count on fewer than 66,000 men while Sherman had taken charge of the combined Union armies in the West and now commanded about 110,000 well-equipped soldiers. A steady stream of fresh troops replenished the blue ranks, while Johnston knew that he would be virtually without recruits or reinforcements in the coming struggle. It was no secret that Sherman's objective was capture of strategically-important Atlanta, and in early May the long-expected Yankee advance began.

There would be one final dress parade in Gist's brigade on May 6, as Janie and her general celebrated their first wedding anniversary before saying good bye for the last time. Breaking camp, the brigade marched through Dalton into

Crow's Valley and took up position in defense of Mill Creek Gap, the nearest pass through Rocky Face Ridge. On the ridge the main Confederate line was strongly posted. Elements of Gist's brigade were involved on the ninth in a "sharp skirmish" at the Gap, before suddenly being sent on an all-night march southward through Dalton to near Resaca.[7]

Johnston placed the bulk of his army into position around Resaca with his flanks resting on the Conasauga and Oostanaula Rivers. Early on the eleventh Gist was ordered to a point about halfway between Resaca and Calhoun, there to watch the Oostanaula crossings at Gideon's Ford and, a mile farther downstream, McGinnis' Ferry. For the next three days he had little to do. Then on the fourteenth word came that the enemy was crossing at McGinnis' Ferry. Sherman had ordered Major General James B. McPherson to march down the west bank of the Oostanaula, jump the river and flank Johnston. Realizing the threat, Gist ordered that the 24th South Carolina march rapidly to the point of danger from their post at Gideon's Ford. When Capers arrived he found the enemy force, backed by artillery, pushing the 16th South Carolina down the road that led to Calhoun. Capers huddled briefly with Colonel James McCullough, commander of the beleaguered regiment, then ordered a charge that succeeded in driving the Federals back to the river. The blue infantry retreated under cover of their artillery on the opposite bank and stayed there. Mission accomplished, Capers marched his regiment back to Gideon's Ford.[8]

All along Gist's front the enemy effort to cross had been a halfhearted affair, perhaps merely a feint. Some three miles farther downstream, where the river took a bend to the west, a much more serious operation was in progress. There at Lay's Ferry the division of Thomas W. Sweeny pushed back Walker's defenders and landed a brigade on the Confederate bank. Late in the day Sweeny was told of Rebels building a bridge and crossing over in great force to cut him off. Apparently he was hearing a badly-distorted version of the repulse at McGinnis' Ferry, but three seemingly-reliable reports compelled him to pull back his exposed brigade. Reconnaissance that night showed no Rebel pursuit, and next morning Sweeny's entire division, now under the command of Colonel Elliott W. Rice, crossed over the river and scattered the opposition.[9]

Unreliable intelligence was not only a Federal problem. Several hours after Sweeny's troops had retreated from their bridgehead, Johnston received word from his cavalry that no fewer than two Union divisions were across at that moment. When Sweeny's division actually did bridge the river next morning Walker at first maintained that all was quiet. Despite the confusion, Johnston knew he must eventually retreat. He had until now successfully grappled with Sherman's frontal assaults, inflicting considerable punishment on the invader. But with battle still raging at his front, for the time being Old Joe felt he needed every man. Late in the afternoon Gist's brigade, rather than being sent to the Lay's Ferry danger point with other units of Walker's division, was ordered to reinforce the center of the Confederate line.[10]

"The roar of battle at Resaca urged our march, and the men moved with alacrity to the duty assigned them," reported Capers. "Here we remained for the rest of the day," he complained, "under fire and in reserve."[11]

Late that night Johnston slipped away southward. "We could not send a force sufficient to beat the force in our rear and at same time hold present position," Johnston's aide tersely confided in his journal. Walker's assignment to hold the Oostanaula line had by now become clearly a case of much too little too late. Greatly outnumbered, some of the Federals armed with new Henry repeating rifles, Walker was only able to slow their advance. By morning of the sixteenth the scattered brigades of Walker's division regrouped on a line that faced the expanding and now unassailable Federal bridgehead.[12]

Before long Rebel pickets were driven back so far that the bivouac area of Hardee's corps came under a galling artillery fire. About 2 p.m. Hardee ordered Walker to clear away the annoying Yankee force and the Georgian turned to Gist. Directing the drama from a small hill, Gist sent forward Colonel Capers' 24th South Carolina in conjunction with the 1st Battalion of Georgia sharpshooters from Stevens' brigade. One observer recalled that he "never saw anything of the kind better done." The Southerners advanced with precision, then on order charged with a Rebel yell. Capers reported that "the enemy, after firing wildly over us, broke into a precipitous retreat, the battery narrowly escaping capture." So far were the enemy driven that Gist became alarmed and sent a courier galloping after Capers to halt his victorious troops before the little command took on the entire Union corps.[13]

Gist's men had demanded and received a little elbow-room. But now Johnston was again on the move southward. Coming to a fork in the road to Adairsville he split his army, knowing that Sherman would do the same. With luck he hoped to quickly reunite his command and crush one of the surprised and outnumbered Union columns near Cassville. "The greatest enthusiasm prevailed in our ranks as the men and officers saw the army formed for battle," remembered Capers. Gist's brigade was on the left of the division, with the 24th South Carolina and the 46th Georgia in the front line and the 16th South Carolina and the 8th Georgia Battalion in the rear. At 2 p.m. on May 19, the front line advanced to within three-fourths mile of the Yankee position. Gist and his men halted in an open field and sweltered in the Georgia sun awaiting orders while the Federals busily prepared to receive their charge. Noticing an abandoned house nearby, Gist ordered sharpshooters to take up position in the second-floor windows.

Far away to the right, Lieutenant General John Bell Hood feared that Union horse soldiers had gotten in his rear, causing Johnston to lose his nerve and finally call off the heralded attack. All this high-level indecision was unknown to Gist, who became increasingly impatient at hearing nothing from his superiors. Riding to the front line, he ordered that at precisely 4 p.m. his regiments end the futile waiting and retire. The hour came, Gist's brigade did an about-face, marched rearward one mile and dug in. Few shots had been fired on either side.[14]

In the middle of the night Gist was awakened with new orders to move out. Johnston was retreating again. The brigade crossed the Etowah River in the darkness, marched about two miles farther and went into bivouac on the Alla-toona Road.[15] While Gist rested there, Sherman cut loose from his railroad lifeline and made another sweep to the west and south.

Johnston shifted to meet him in the woods surrounding a little Methodist house of worship called New Hope Church. The Yankees learned to call it "the hell hole." When one frontal attack floundered, Sherman tried to surprise the Confederate flank and ran into the gleaming bayonets of Pat Cleburne's warriors. Sherman would regret these four bloody days of failure and agony. Though held in reserve, Gist's brigade took a few casualties, and with the rest of the Rebel army followed Sherman's retreat northeastward.[16]

The Union commander was once again secure astraddle his railroad. But looking to the south he found the way blocked by Rebels firmly holding Brush Mountain on the right, Lost Mountain on the left and Pine Mountain in the center. Two miles farther back stood even more formidable Kennesaw Mountain, by now fairly bristling with Confederate cannon.

Gist was first posted in rear of Pine Mountain, then on June 19 ordered to positions at the south and west of Kennesaw Mountain, on Burnt Hickory Road. His brigade formed the right of Hardee's corps, with Samuel French's division of Polk's corps to his right on a prominence called Pigeon Hill. The men spent the few hours granted them digging in the red Georgia clay. The breastworks they fashioned were fronted in the direction of the enemy with great pine logs and approaches were studded with obstructions.[17]

On the twentieth the Yankees appeared, established their lines about 300 yards from Gist and immediately tangled with Rebel pickets. Summer rainstorms drenched the men while they dodged constant artillery and rifle fire. Four days later, in a major show of strength, the Federals tried to drive in the brigade's hard-pressed picket line. Gist called on the reliable 24th South Carolina, which pushed back the assaulting force. With perhaps a hint of admiration, Capers reported capturing a Yankee sharpshooter during the skirmish "who had a small looking-glass attached to the butt of his musket, so that he could sit behind his breast-work, perfectly protected, with his back to us, and by looking into his glass, sight along the barrel of his piece."[18]

By June 27 the preliminaries were over. Determined to take advantage of his superior numbers, Sherman sought to overwhelm Johnston on Kennesaw Mountain in a crushing frontal assault. Atlanta would then be his for the taking. Early morning began with the thunder of Union artillery. At 9:30 came a general advance along the entire ten-mile front as wave after blue wave swept forward against the mountain in a seemingly irrestible flood. But this was not to be a repeat of the Missionary Ridge debacle. Tens of thousands of Southern rifles and hundreds of cannon answered the Union challenge, transforming Kennesaw's peaks into an erupting volcano of death.

It soon became clear that the Union attack had two targets. One was two miles south of the mountain where Major Generals Cleburne and Benjamin F. Cheatham proved to be immovable barriers in Sherman's path. The other thrust was aimed directly at Pigeon Hill, the objective being to split the Confederate army at that point. Here for two and one-half hours one Yankee charge after another came straight at Gist's brigade, each one cut to pieces and driven back by fire from his veterans, assisted by artillery on the heights to the right,[19]

All along the Kennesaw line the Federals were bloodily repulsed. Realizing his miscalculation, Sherman pulled back the survivors, putting an end to the carnage. Johnston had suffered only 808 casualties while Sherman's losses were almost four times that number. Down on Gist's line the enemy dug in just 100 yards away, making a picket line impossible. For another week constant fire made life miserable for the troops on both sides.[20]

After accumulating sufficient supplies to again cut loose from the railroad, Sherman on July 2 began another flanking maneuver, bypassing Kennesaw Mountain. That night Gist and his troops retired to near Smyrna Church, five miles south of Marietta.[21] Johnston set to work building strong fortifications north of the Chattahoochie River, confidently expecting to hold the line there many weeks.

A few days later Sherman surprised him with an upstream crossing of the river. The invader was now in the very suburbs of Atlanta, throwing the city into near panic. Politicians and citizens cried to President Davis for a change in command. What little confidence the President retained in the General was undermined by a series of secret communications from corps commander Hood, inditing Johnston as incompetent. After consulting with Lee and the cabinet, Davis telegraphed Johnston one more time for his plans. Receiving what he took to be a defeatist reply, on July 18 the President made Hood a full general and placed him in command of Johnston's army.

To the troops, losing Johnston was a disaster. His popularity had never declined within the army, despite the ground he had given up. Though forced to retreat, the army had never been beaten in battle and Gist could still brag of his troop's *espirit de corps*. Gist's brigade with Walker's division was marching past Johnston's headquarters on the Marietta Road, having just heard the bitter news of Old Joe's downfall. The officers turned to salute their chief and the men removed hats in silent tribute.[22]

If Johnston was condemned as overly cautious, no such charge could be brought against John Bell Hood. Just three months older than Gist, the Kentuckian graduated from the

United States Military Academy in 1853 and served on the frontier during the years before the war. "Sam" Hood's career in Confederate gray had been brilliant and his promotion meteoric. Personally fearless, his arm was crippled at Gettysburg and Chickamauga cost him a leg. Whatever the odds or the risks involved, under Hood the Army of Tennessee would retreat no further. "He is brave," wrote Walker to his wife, "whether he has the capacity to command armies (for it requires a high order of talent) time will divulge..."[23]

Gist's brigade went into bivouac east of Peachtree Road some three miles north of the city. Probably because of the losses suffered in bearing the brunt of the fighting at Kennesaw Mountain, Gist had been reinforced a week earlier by elements of a disbanded brigade. Added to his command were the 2nd Battalion of Georgia Sharpshooters and three understrength regiments: the 65th Georgia, the 5th Mississippi and 8th Mississippi. At midday on the nineteenth Gist's men relieved Alexander Reynolds' brigade on a line south of Peachtree Creek.[24]

Union Major General John M. Schofield had shared a room with Hood at West Point and remembered his old friend's temperament. He warned Sherman to expect an attack momentarily, but perhaps never expected himself how swiftly it would come. The very day after assuming command, Hood set a plan in motion. Learning of a gap in the alignment of the advancing wings of the enemy, he determined to first destroy Thomas' army astride Peachtree Creek, then turn on the remainder of Sherman's forces. At his headquarters in downtown Atlanta Hood spread out maps and issued orders to his three corps commanders. To Hardee would go the honor of attacking Thomas.

Though the assault was set for 1 p.m., not until three hours later was all in readiness. Foot-dragging had allowed most of Thomas' troops to cross Peachtree Creek. The badly-handled offensive, when it came, did catch the Yankees off guard and initially threw them back. Sherman himself described the Confederate attack as "furious" and "bold."

But Hardee allowed his troops to attack piecemeal, some never coming in contact with the enemy at all. There was none of the precise timing called for in the commanding General's textbook-perfect plan. Gist's brigade faced Union Major General Joseph Hooker's XX Corps and experienced fierce fighting before being forced to fall back with the rest of the Southern army.[25]

Within forty-eight hours Hood would try again. East of Atlanta Union General McPherson's flank was thought to be dangerously exposed and here Hardee's corps was again ordered to attack, though the men were exhausted from two days of fighting and marching. The divisions of Walker and Bate would come in from the extreme right and hit the Federals from the rear while Cleburne and Maney rolled up the end of the blue line. But this time the Confederates were the ones surprised. The enemy flank was not "in the air" as expected, but entrenched and ready. Walker's division was delayed as the men struggled through the woods. At one point Gist, "more familiar with the ground" according to one officer, and seeing a tactical advantage to be gained, briefly halted the advance. Walker came up and demanded "in strong terms" that the division continue forward. Just then a blue-clad rifleman spotted Walker on horseback, took aim and fired, killing the forty-seven year old Georgian.

Since two of Hardee's divisions (Maney's on the left and Bate's on the right) were delayed in arriving at their assign-ed positions, the attack had to be made about 1 p.m. by the divisions of Walker and Cleburne alone. The brigade of Walker's division farthest to the right, commanded by independent-minded Colonel Nisbet, aligned itself with the tardy Bate and was lost to its own division. Depleted by one brigade, unsupported on the right and with their experienc-ed commander dead, Walker's division went forward with a shout. They never fought with greater fury, but a devastating fire cut through their ranks. "Gist's attack though gallant was entirely without support," remembered an officer, "and the enemy rallying held the front which we approached within

100 yards and by enfilade fire of musketry and artillery sent us back broken..." Gist himself received a painful wound in the hand that finally forced him to turn over command of the brigade to Colonel James McCullough of the 16th South Carolina. The General stayed on the field however, making his way to the hospital only later. In mid-afternoon he was witness to the death of his young aide, Lieutenant Joseph Clay Habersham, torn to pieces by an exploding shell.[26]

Bate's overdue assault, when it finally came, was also repulsed. Subsequent attempts during the long afternoon to crack the Union line each time met with failure. Almost as an afterthought, Cheatham's corps was ordered out of Atlanta's trenches late in the day. Their frontal assault pushed the Federals back without breaking them. Hardee's men, said Sherman, "attacked boldly and repeatedly," but the Union commander was bewildered by Hood's failure to coordinate his offensive and attack simultaneously with Cheatham.[27] Confederates were wondering the same thing. Sherman had lost 3,722 men in the Battle of Atlanta, Hood nearly 8,000.

The horrendous losses, and the death of General Walker, made major reorganization necessary. On July 24 Walker's old division was broken up and its component brigades distributed to the other divisions of Hardee's corps. Gist lost the 5th and 8th Mississippi after their brief service under him, and his brigade was reassigned to Cheatham's division.[28]

Sherman still lacked the manpower to surround Atlanta, and ten miles of massive earthworks convinced him he dare not risk storming the city. Shrewdly he decided to strike for Hood's remaining railroad lifeline to the west. In the Battle of Ezra Church on July 28, Atlanta's defenders saved the Macon and Western Railroad, but at a terrible cost. In just ten days as commander, Hood had lost nearly a third of his army.

Frustrated that Atlanta still eluded his grasp, Sherman unleashed artillery against the civilians remaining in the embattled city. "Let us destroy Atlanta and make it a desolation," ordered the hard-eyed conqueror as he called for heavy siege guns to be sent by rail from Chattanooga. Over the next few weeks 5,000 Yankee shells screamed into the city, killing and maiming indiscriminately. In response to protests that innocent noncombatants were suffering, Sherman shot back that they could leave. Some did. Many more burrowed into their yards and bravely tried to adapt to a world gone mad.[29]

Terrifying though it was, cannon fire alone could not bring Atlanta to her knees. Sherman concluded that he must gamble to break the siege. Flanking movements during the spring and summer campaign had succeeded in forcing the Rebels to retreat. It might work again. On August 26 the people of Atlanta and her defenders awoke to an eerie silence. News quickly spread that the Yankees had gone! Some dared hope that Sherman — his lines of supply stretched to the breaking point — had abandoned the siege and retreated northward. Hood feared the worst and sent Hardee's corps south of Atlanta to Jonesboro. True to form, Sherman had boldly set in motion 60,000 men swinging southwestward to sever Hood's remaining railroad link.

By now Gist was out of the hospital and with the troops in Jonesboro, though he still had not returned to duty. His brigade was commanded by Colonel McCullough while General Maney temporarily had charge of Cheatham's division.[30] On August 31 Sherman's soldiers siezed Rough and Ready, a village on the railroad halfway between Atlanta and Jonesboro, and cut the telegraph lines linking Hood and Hardee. The same day just to the west of Jonesboro, Maney formed his division in support of Bate's and Cleburne's divisions. The Union army in great strength had crossed the Flint River, menacing the very survival of Atlanta.

When the two leading Rebel divisions attacked and were thrown back, Maney was ordered to cancel his assault and late that night the division withdrew to Jonesboro. By early afternoon September 1 the Yankees had pushed far to the east above Jonesboro, forcing Hardee to conform. To this new position went Gist's brigade, command of which had passed to Colonel Capers. Hardee arrived and placed the brigade astride the railroad cut and ordered their breastworks made as strong as possible. Late that afternoon the enemy attacked furiously, were repulsed, then came on again. In desperate fighting Capers' troops wavered for a time, then rallied and held the line.[31]

Hardee personally thanked the Colonel for the brigade's gallant conduct, even as he planned their retreat.[32] The Lieutenant General began to realize that his corps confronted practically Sherman's entire army, still advancing to the east and threatening his destruction. During the night Hardee began to pull his exhausted men from the Jonesboro lines and send them southward to safety at Lovejoy's Station. Hood also bowed to the inevitable. To save the army he abandoned Atlanta, destroyed his stockpile of ammunition and supplies, and by a circuitous route to the east and south marched to join forces with Hardee at Lovejoy's.

It was an orderly withdrawal. Still convalescing and without a command, Gist was down by the Jonesboro tracks as the wounded were loaded aboard the cars. At about 3 a.m., September 2, Yankee skirmishers burst into town, the advance guard of Brigadier General William Harrow's division. The train loaded with wounded pulled out just in time to avoid capture, and Gist kept himself from becoming a prisoner of war by scrambling aboard. He counted himself fortunate to have lost only two horses, a servant and baggage. Wiley Howard, the General's loyal body servant, with his master evaded capture.[33]

While the Confederates dug in at Lovejoy's Station, Gist, on or about his thirty-third birthday, returned to duty as temporary commander of Cheatham's division. He defiantly chose a position fewer than two miles from Yankee-occupied Jonesboro. Military necessity would dictate a cautious reconnaissance. Gist in fact directed an aggressive probing and skirmishing that perhaps reflected his frustration.[34] He seemed to be shaking his fist at the conquerors of Atlanta, daring them to think he was whipped.

It was a spirit shared by his commanding general. Though much reduced in strength, the Army of Tennessee was still a force to be reckoned with. Already Hood was formulating a strategy.

Chapter Eleven
"I Might Get Tripped Up This Evening"

Sherman had barely entered Atlanta when the remaining civilians were shocked by his decree that the city be forcibly depopulated. The battered survivors of the siege must now become homeless refugees. Hood agreed to an armistice of ten days to facilitate the evacuation, but protested vehemently the cruelty of the measure. Sherman lashed back in a heated exchange that accomplished nothing except to further establish himself as an uncompromising exponent of total war.

With the expiration of the truce Hood shifted his headquarters some twenty-five miles westward to Palmetto, Georgia. Cheatham returned to command of his division, and Gist to his brigade,[1] while the men made ready for a review by the President of the Confederacy. With the fall of Atlanta, many had lost heart. War-weary Georgia wavered and Davis felt his presence and words might help revive spirits.

Morale in the army suffered as well. "General Johnston is all that is desired," wrote Lieutenant James A. Tillman of the 24th South Carolina to his brother on September 25. "The whole army would hail his return with the wildest shouts of applause, and yet our President will not reinstate him." Tillman expected the commander-in-chief's reception to be icy since Davis "has forfeited all claims to our regard and kind consideration." The Lieutenant caustically predicted that "hurrahs for Johnston will greet his ears."

In many of the commands reviewed by the chief executive that day it was indeed the insubordinate cry he heard. Gist's brigade "moved out sullenly, to be seen by him," continued Tillman.

> We had scarcely taken position before his Excellency appeared and rode slowly along the line, saluting officers and men by raising his hat as he passed by. Though scarcely a man left the bivouac who had not determined to treat him coldly, his calm pale face and frosty locks created a deep sympathy in behalf of the careworn Executive, and when General Gist proposed "three cheers for our President" a wild, united shout was given, such as we used to give when our great and much loved General was with us and rode along the line or encampment.[2]

Returning Johnston to the army was not an option in the President's mind. Despite the loss of Atlanta, Hood had at least proven himself a fighter and a man who would not accept defeat. Davis met with his general and together they agreed to a new strategy. .The Army of Tennessee would march to the north and west around Atlanta, severing Sherman's rail link to Chattanooga. If his adversary left the Atlanta fortifications in pursuit, Hood could fight if the opportunity seemed favorable or pull back into Alabama if badly outnumbered. Should Hood score a victory against Sherman he could consider advancing farther northward into Tennessee. But if the Yankees moved south out of Atlanta, Davis was insistent that Hood closely follow. Georgia was not to be adandoned to Sherman's depradations.

The President approved Hardee's transfer after conflict erupted between Hood and his corps commander. Cheatham moved up to take charge of Hardee's corps while command of the division went temporarily to Gist.[3]

The army broke camp at Palmetto at the end of the month and by the first week in October was back at the scenes of summer's struggles. As the Rebels marched northward, Lieutenant General Alexander P. Stewart's corps demolished the railroad that fed Sherman's army resting in Atlanta. Sherman gave chase, but soon tired of the futile effort to secure his supply lines. "It will be a physical impossibility to protect the roads," he complained to Grant, "now that Hood...and the whole batch of devils are turned loose without home or habitation."[4] What Sherman proposed was cutting free from his supply lines, abandoning Atlanta and marching for the coast. The risks of living off the land seemed not as burdensome as playing Hood's game by remaining on the defensive. All Sherman lacked was the permission of his superiors.

Gist returned to leadership of his brigade on the ninth, permanent command of the division going to John C. Brown. "How is it B[rown] ranks Gist?" asked a correspondent of Colonel Capers. After all, Gist's date of rank preceded Brown's by several months and the South Carolinian had by experience and performance proven himself eminently qualified to command a division. Gist and his friends could not help but note that Brown was a Tennessean, reminding them of the Bate promotion that kept Gist from advancement in February.[5]

On the thirteenth the army arrived at Dalton and Hood sent an ultimatum to the Yankee garrison's commander. Brown's division was ordered into position to assault the stronghold, a show of force that proved sufficient to secure the surrender of the nearly 1,000 Federals. Gist spent that afternoon and morning of the next day helping tear up twenty miles of track from Dalton to Tunnel Hill.[6]

By October 16 Sherman was in pursuit with some 40,000 men. The 24th South Carolina of Gist's brigade was called on to delay the Yankee advance at Ship's Gap while Hood slipped away. Capers made his troop dispositions as best he could, reporting to Gist that seventeen enemy regimental flags were counted in his front. Gist sent a courier back to the Colonel cautioning him to hold the Gap as long as possible, but without sacrificing his little command. The regiment stood unsupported against an entire Federal division. In hard fighting two of Capers' most advanced companies, A and F, were cut off and half their officers and men captured. The remainder of the regiment got away, firing as they withdrew, to rejoin Gist's brigade on the Summerville Road. Sherman in his memoirs specifically remembered the gallant 24th, "which had been left there to hold us in check." The Union commander lamented the delay that insured Hood's withdrawal. "I hoped to catch him and force him to battle; but by the time we had got enough troops across the mountain at Ship's Gap, Hood had escaped..."[7]

There at Ship's Gap the Union commander was handed a coded message that did much to raise his spirits. Washington was inclined to approve his plan of a march to the seacoast. Over the next few weeks Sherman dispatched two corps under Major Generals David Stanley and John Schofield to join forces with Thomas in Nashville. This army, Sherman felt certain, would be capable of dealing with the unpredictable Hood, leaving him free to lay waste to Georgia.

Hood by mid-October had begun to deviate from the strategy so recently worked out with the President, evidencing no willingness at all to fight Sherman or stay within striking distance of the Yankees in Georgia. The Confederate commander in fact had begun to conjure grandiose plans for his little army. Davis had tried to encourage the people with talk of eventually liberating Tennessee and Kentucky, but to him that was dependent on first defeating Sherman. Now Hood dreamed of advancing all the way to the Ohio River, perhaps invading the North or joining forces with Lee to smash Grant in Virginia. He was retreating from reality. Hood's frustration in defeat was intensified by his painful wounds and emotional turmoil over a failing romance. In his anguish the General sought to shift blame for every setback. At Jonesboro he accused the men in the ranks of cowardice. Always one to measure gallantry in terms of casualty figures, Hood came to doubt his army's offensive prowess. He repeatedly taunted his lieutenants with what for him became an obsession: The men had lost their willingness to charge breastworks. For Hood the answer was to drive fear out of them in a morale-boosting attack.

Marching northwestward across Alabama, Hood made feeble attempts to resupply his army. The weather was turning cold and wet and there were men in Gist's brigade tramping barefoot through the mud. Arriving in the Tennessee Valley region of northern Alabama, the men contrasted the beauty of the countryside with the devastation left by the enemy. On the eve of crossing into the Volunteer State, Hood issued a proclamation to his troops, in Capers' words "exhorting every man and officer resolutely to vow the redemption of Tennessee from the grasp of the foe." Gist's veterans received the message with enthusiasm, "though many of the gallant soldiers who cheered were absolutely suffering for clothing and shoes." With bands playing, on Sunday, November 13 Gist's brigade crossed the Tennessee River on a pontoon bridge. At one village a party of admiring ladies, "many of them pretty," in Colonel Capers' words, asked to be introduced to Generals Gist and Brown as they and their retinue of staff officers rode through. The brigade continued marching northward in a snowstorm that made the roads so muddy the soldiers preferred to trudge through the woods and fields. Spirits were high, despite the cold weather and scanty food. At one point the men were reduced to a ration of nothing more than dried corn. By the time they reached Columbia, Tennessee their daily diet had "improved" to three biscuits per man.[8]

It may have been about this time that Gist learned of Atlanta's fate. Before beginning his march to the sea, Sherman saw to it that the city was systematically destroyed.

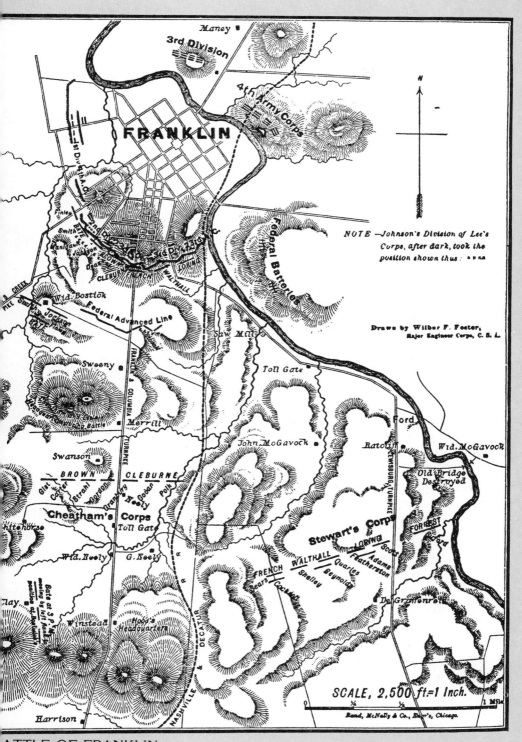

BATTLE OF FRANKLIN
(Battles and Leaders of the Civil War)

Yankee engineers devised a battering ram that thundered up and down streets, turning brick structures into rubble and dust. The once-proud city was then put to the torch, beginning a conflagration that would take four days to burn itself out. To the strain of "John Brown's Body," Sherman then moved south into the nearly-undefended Georgia countryside.

The Federal troops left behind to deal with Hood were racing to a rendezvous with Thomas at heavily-fortified Nashville. The Union column under Schofield stood between Hood's forces and the Tennessee capital with orders to slow, if possible, the Confederate advance. With Major General Nathan Bedford Forrest's cavalry leading the way, on November 29 Cheatham's corps crossed the Duck River at Davis' Ford and in a forced march reached Spring Hill late in the day. Now in Schofield's rear, the Rebel commander had positioned himself to deliver a crushing blow to the Federals. Cheatham planned an assault that would begin on the right, led off by Brown's division. At the sound of the guns, Cleburne and then Bate would in turn send their divisions forward. Expecting success, but leaving the details to subordinates, Hood retired to the rear.

There in the enveloping darkness, Gist waited with his brigade the order to advance. The enemy could be heard in confused and noisy flight up the pike toward Franklin. Still no orders came from Brown. Gist could not understand what was happening. Victory was there for the taking. Why was he not allowed to unleash his veterans against the retreating enemy? Burning with impatience, Gist and fellow brigade commander Otho Strahl rode in the direction of the Yankees, accompanied by Colonel Capers. In the bitterly-cold twilight they knew the quarry was slipping from their grasp. Whether spoken or not, it must have occurred to each officer that but for politics Gist might be commanding the division that night. As they turned to gallop back to their lines the frustration became too much for Capers. Drawing his revolver, he fired until the pistol was empty at the voices he heard in the darkness.[9]

Still Brown hesitated. He was paralyzed by fear for his flanks. He misunderstood his orders. Confronted by his brigadiers, the General was uncommunicative and touchy.[10] Cheatham too, seemed to have lost his resolve as a splendid opportunity slipped away.

Back in his own lines, Gist lay down on the ground to rest, his head on his saddle. Before long Wiley Howard, the General's versatile servant, returned to camp. "I was ridin' Joe Johnston, one of General Gist's best horses," explained Wiley. "He was mighty good to me, and he knew I was good to his horses."

The General's indispensable friend had been on what was apparently a two-or-three-day foraging expedition. "I asked him how he was getting on?" Wiley continued. "He said he was mighty hungry and wanted me to get something for him to eat as soon as possible. He asked what I had, and I says chicken, and hominy, and biscuit. He says that was just what he wanted. And when I got their supper, he and the other gentlemen with him, ate mighty hearty."[11]

Early next morning the army moved out on the Franklin Pike, Stewart's corps leading the way. Cheatham's indolence and Hood's disengaged attitude throughout the previous day's affair made Brown's failure their own. The tormented army commander, by now clearly unfit for duty, lashed out at everyone, including the men in the ranks. In Hood's clouded mind he commanded cowards. Only one remedy would suffice: the hard discipline of a frontal assault.

A roadside littered with burned wagons and dead mules told of the hurried Yankee flight northward to Franklin. In contrast to the biting cold that had caused so much suffering earlier in the month, this last day of November was proving bright and pleasant. Perhaps Confederate fortunes would improve as well. By early afternoon Stewart's corps pushed Schofield's rear guard from a range of hills that crossed the pike and there Hood formed his men in line of battle. There would be no waiting for Lieutenant General Stephen D. Lee's corps and the artillery to come up. And Forrest could not

persuade his commander to consider the wisdom of a flanking maneuver. Hood was determined to purge his men of
their "timidity" then and there. Tragically ignorant of
Thomas' massive army then gathering at Nashville, Hood was
under the impression that Schofield's was the only force
standing between him and the liberation of Tennessee. Victory at Franklin and the way was open to the Ohio.

Now fewer than two miles apart, the opposing armies
were fairly evenly matched. But Schofield's Federals would
not be relying for protection on hastily-thrown-up field fortifications. Franklin rested in a bend of the Harpeth River
and for many months had been encircled by extensive and
well-prepared earthworks. An advanced line, manned by two
Yankee brigades, stood several hundred yards in front of the
main fortifications and Federal batteries were posted to
sweep the treeless, level field. Considering their obvious
strength, many Northerners expressed disbelief that the
Rebels would dare attempt to storm Franklin.

Gist calmly ate dinner, and as he finished turned to Wiley
and confirmed that a fight was imminent. "Wiley, you take
charge of my money, my watch and my ring. I might get tripped up this evening. If I do, take care of those things. Use
what money you need, and if anything happens, take the
watch and ring to your Miss Janie."

"Now, you had better saddle Joe. Kitty is broke down,"
continued the General.

"Marse States, you ain't got no business riding Joe," protested Wiley. "Joe ain't got no sense when the bullets come
around."

Gist was firm. Kitty was stumbling and he would have
to take a chance on Joe, even if the animal was skittish in
battle. "He'll have to get used to the bullets," concluded the
General.

"I didn't say no more," remembered Wiley, "for when
Marse States talked that way, twarn't no use."[12]

Hood's men marched in formation over the crest of the
hill, Stewart's corps on the right of the road and Cheatham's

on the left. Brown's division was in the center of the corps, flanked by Cleburne and Bate. Brown would send his division forward two brigades deep, and into the front line he ordered Generals Gist and George Gordon.[13]

It was nearly four o'clock. Somewhere a regimental band struck up "The Bonnie Blue Flag." In the Indian summer afternoon the banners of Gist's brigade waved bravely, the same colors presented by Beauregard to the regiments that spring day so long ago.

The panorama was forever imprinted on the memory of Colonel Capers:

> Just before the charge was ordered the brigade passed over an elevation, from which we beheld the magnificent spectacle the battlefield presented — bands were playing, general and staff officers and gallant couriers were riding in front of and between the lines, 100 battle-flags were waving in the smoke of battle, and bursting shells were wreathing the air with great circles of smoke, while 20,000 brave men were marching in perfect order against the foe. The sight inspired every man of the Twenty-fourth with the sentiment of duty... General Gist, attended by Capt. H. D. Garden and Lieut. Frank Trenholm, of his staff, rode down our front, and returning, ordered the charge, in concert with General Gordon. In passing from the left to the right of the regiment the general waved his hat to us, expressed his pride and confidence in the Twenty-fourth, and rode away in the smoke of battle, never more to be seen by the men he had commanded on so many fields.[14]

From his vantage point Wiley saw the brigade cross a small creek and halt briefly at a low rock wall before breaking into a charge. Under deadly rifle and artillery fire they headed straight for those two advanced Union brigades. Wiley's fears were realized when Gist's horse was wounded. "Joe had been shot through the neck, and was rearing and plunging so he had to dismount... The last time I saw Marse States he was on foot, near a sugar maple tree, still leading his men."[15]

"We poured a very destructive fire into their line and it staggered them very much," reported Yankee Colonel Joseph Conrad.[16] Gist was in front and to the right of his brigade when one of those bullets struck him in the thigh. He refused to leave the field and as his men reached the enemy breastworks he was hit again. This time the .58 caliber lead missile tore into his chest, piercing the right lung. In great pain Gist was carried by litter bearers to the field hospital, accompanied by his aide. "Lieutenant Trenholm, take me home to my wife," were his only words. At first his suffering was intense, but as the hours passed the agony seemed to lessen. Dr. Wright, a friend of the General, did all that he could.

Few of Gist's men were close enough to see their General go down. Overrunning the advanced enemy position, they literally chased the fleeing bluecoats back into the main Union line to plant the flags of Gist's brigade on the very parapet. There they grappled hand-to-hand with the enemy in one of the bloodiest combats of the war. As darkness fell the surviving Confederate attackers lacked the strength to break through, but were too stubborn to fall back. Vicious fighting continued into the night.

For States Rights Gist the fury of battle raged far away, its outcome the burden of others. To the doctor he spoke but little. "Take me to my wife," he whispered again. It was a plea as simple as it was eloquent, a prayer no power on earth could now fulfill. He died at 8:30 p.m.[17]

Late in the night Wiley heard talk that his master had fallen and he set out in search. "It took me a long time to make my way. The ground was piled with wounded men and with dead men. Sometimes I stopped and did what I could." In the pre-dawn darkness he found the hospital and sadly learned the truth from Dr. Wright.[18] By morning news of the General's death began to reach the remnants of his brigade on the parapet.

Around midnight the Yankees had pulled out of Franklin and headed for the security of Nashville, leaving their dead and seriously wounded behind. In possession of the field of battle, Hood claimed victory. Still out of touch with reality, the commander had decimated his army, sacrificing 7,000 irreplaceable men. In the officer corps the casualties were staggering. The Army of Tennessee had lost twelve generals, six of them killed or mortally wounded. Besides Gist, dead or dying were Cleburne, Strahl, John Adams, Hiram Granbury and John Carter. The holocaust left Gist's once powerful brigade a shattered band commanded by a captain.[19]

Survivors spent the day burying the dead. Thousands would be laid side-by-side in long trenches, a torn piece of blanket placed over each face before the mass grave was filled with dirt. Dr. Wright found no coffin, but was able to secure a cedar box in which to bury General Gist. The doctor also borrowed an army ambulance.

The small party accompanying the General's body drove to the William White residence on the far western side of the battlefield, close by the family burying ground. Wiley pulled up to the gate and met Mrs. White at the door. "I told her General Gist had been killed, and asked her if we could bury him in her graveyard. She said that for such a man she could not do enough." She instructed that a panel of the fence be knocked out so that the ambulance could back up to the front door. General Gist's body was then brought inside and laid on the parlor sofa while Mrs. White sent for her preacher. There in the Whites' yard, under a large cedar tree, a funeral was held with military honors. All of Gist's regiments were represented. "All of the officers were there — that is, all that was left. It was a sad time to them."[20]

Soon after the battle, rumors began to reach South Carolina that Gist was among the dead, though not for several days was it officially confirmed. The agonizing news reached Janie at Live Oak Plantation. "Words cannot depict her great sorrow," editorialized the *Charleston Daily Courier.* "Her grief is sacred, and we would not intrude upon its sanctity."

"The river of blood rolls on," lamented the Charleston writer, "growing deeper and wider and sweeping away the young, the manful, the gifted, and the brave." Gist, said the newspaper, "possessed a strong, clear, quick intellect; a sound judgement; an earnest, determined spirit...Adorned with those high traits and virtues, he rendered good service to the cause in whose vindication he gave his life..."[21]

In Columbia, Mary Chesnut learned that Gist had been killed gallantly leading his men. She felt the indignation rising within as she wrote in her journal. "One of Mr. Chesnut's sins, thrown in his teeth by the legislature of South Carolina, was that he procured the promotion of Gist — States Rights Gist — by his influence in Richmond. What have these comfortable stay-at-home patriots to say of General Gist now!"[22]

Partisanship seemed for the moment forgotten at the State House. Henry Buist of Charleston eulogized Gist as "earnest in purpose, patriotic in impulse, chivalrous in sentiment..." The words of old unionist Benjamin F. Perry seemed to carry special weight. Perry had opposed secession in 1860, yet his political views never prejudiced his personal relationships. Now he rose from his desk to speak of his young friend.

> I concur with all my heart in this tribute...He was one of South Carolina's most gallant and promising sons. I heard a distinguished Colonel of his brigade say that he was the wisest officer in council that he had ever met. It was my fortune to have known General Gist early in his life, and then formed a high estimate of his character and talents. His rapid promotion and success did not surprise me...Had his life been spared he would soon have risen higher...[Janie Gist's] only consolation is that he fell in the defense of his bleeding country, gloriously leading his command to victory and death! Though cut off in the opening prime of his manhood, yet he lived long enough to win for himself a name and a fame which his family and State may well be proud of. His brigade was warmly and devotedly attached to him, as I well know through the Greenville regiment of

volunteers, which was part of his command. He had too, the respect and confidence of his superior officers. His fine person, accomplished manners, high talents and heroic courage, could but win the respect, admiration and love of all those with whom he was associated.[23]

Perhaps Wiley expressed it best. "His men thought there was nobody like General Gist. He had a strict way of commanding, but he was mighty kind to them and he had learnt 'em how to fight mighty well."[24]

Epilogue

Final defeat for the Southern cause was only months away. Hood marched the remnants of his army to Nashville, there to be overwhelmed. Sherman by February was wreaking vengeance on the Palmetto State, devastating all in his path including the capital city of Columbia. Now virtually undefended, the "Cradle of Secession" would be shown no mercy.

Down at Live Oak Plantation, Janie was preparing for church when she heard the shouted warning that Yankees were in the neighborhood. While her mother buried the silver under a hedge, the young widow and her terrified sisters secreted themselves in the attic. There in heart-pounding silence they heard rude footsteps and loud voices far below. The blue-clad invaders trampled the shrubbery, stole a piano cover and burned 500 bales of cotton in the gin house. Miraculously, inexplicably, the Adams home was spared. The girls trapped in the attic likely would have been unable to escape had it burned.[1]

For many months survival was the chief concern of most, including Janie Gist. By the spring of 1866 rebuilding was under way as citizens struggled out of the chaos and upheaval of defeat. The young widow felt it was time to bring her husband's remains home for burial. Since he now belonged to all South Carolina, it was only appropriate that the graveyard of Trinity Episcopal Church in the center of the

Grave of General Gist, Trinity Episcopal Church, Columbia.
His epitaph reads, *"He fulfilled the hero's and the patriot's part."*
(Photograph by David Cisco)

Capital City be his final resting place. Colonel Joseph F. Gist made arrangements for the General's body to be disinterred, transferred to a metallic coffin and shipped from Tennessee. The Colonel also ordered a costly monument of Italian marble for the new grave site.[2]

The Columbia *Phoenix* had been urging that a day be set aside each year to memoralize the Confederate dead and suggested the tenth of May, since that was the anniversary of the death of Stonewall Jackson. Perhaps Janie Gist had this in mind as she invited relatives, friends and acquaintances to gather on May 10 at the church for a 10 a.m. funeral service.[3] There under the watchful eye of Federal troops, South Carolina quietly paid her final respects to the General.

The young widow relied on the help of brother-in-law John Hampden Brooks in settling the estate, a task complicated by the fact that there was no will. In common with most Southerners, the war had ruined the fortunes of the Gist family. Claims against the General's estate were heavy and he left little except one thoroughbred horse and the books and furniture in his Union law office. The insolvent estate would remain a burden for many years.[4]

1866 was another year of grief for Janie Gist. Just five days after the General's funeral, her twenty-two year old sister Laura died in childbirth. In October she lost her sister Mary Brooks. "With no profession, heavily in debt, and with a family to support," Captain Brooks carried on alone for two years. It probably came as no surprise to family and friends when he and Janie Gist in 1868 announced their intention to marry. Until her death in 1911 she cherished the Confederate cause and the memory of States Rights Gist, the man who shared her life so briefly.[5]

On the grounds of the State House in Columbia, just across from the spires of Trinity Church, stands South Carolina's monument to her Confederate dead. It honors men the inscription describes as "TRUE TO THE INSTINCTS OF THEIR BIRTH, FAITHFUL TO THE TEACHINGS OF THEIR FATHERS, CON-

STANT IN THEIR LOVE FOR THE STATE..."

LET THE SOUTH CAROLINIAN
OF ANOTHER GENERATION
REMEMBER
THAT THE STATE TAUGHT THEM
HOW TO LIVE AND HOW TO DIE,
AND THAT FROM HER BROKEN FORTUNES
SHE HAS PRESERVED FOR HER CHILDREN
THE PRICELESS TREASURES OF HER MEMORIES,
TEACHING ALL WHO MAY CLAIM
THE SAME BIRTHRIGHT
THAT TRUTH, COURAGE AND PATRIOTISM
ENDURE FOREVER.[6]

Such was the legacy of States Rights Gist.

Bust of States Rights Gist in the South Caroliniana Library, Columbia. The General is remembered with a bust at Vicksburg battlefield and has a street named in his honor in Franklin, Tennessee.
(Photograph by David Cisco)

Janie Margaret Brooks. General Gist's widow wrote in 1911,
"I have always felt that scant justice has been done the General..."
(From Margaret Middleton, <u>Live Oak Plantation</u>)

Appendix One
The Death of General Gist

There are no eyewitness accounts of Gist's death.

The most complete chronicle of the General's last day, his death and burial, is that of Wiley Howard. Howard's convincing narrative has been essential to this researcher's reconstruction of what happened. He is careful to differentiate between what he saw and what he was told the morning after the battle. The richly-detailed report was accepted by the family and is highly accurate in every verifiable particular.[1]

Ellison Capers was himself seriously wounded at Franklin and recounted what he heard later of Gist's death. His story is similar to Howard's except that Capers was under the impression that the General died "almost instantly" after being "shot thro' the heart." As he also quotes Gist's last words, the Colonel surely did not intend "shot thro' the heart" be taken in a literal sense.[2]

Janie Gist mentions the General's leg wound, a detail she may have heard from Trenholm or others.[3]

The *Charleston Daily Courier* reported the initial injury was in the thigh. Their report of the mortal wound being to the "right lung" is undoubtedly more clinically accurate than the "shot thro' the heart" hyperbole. The newspaper also quoted the General's last words.[4]

James T. Williams, an enlisted man in Gist's brigade, in a 1929 letter mentions Gist's last words being directed to Lieutenant Trenholm. Williams stated this information was given him the day after the battle.[5]

Romantic embellishment in some accounts, such as Gist's horse leaping onto the enemy defenses, seems apocryphal at best.[6] Sam Watkins imagining Gist lying dead "with his sword reaching across the breastworks still grasped in his hand," has the ring of the sentimental and overdone. Watkins frankly hero-worshiped "the noble, generous, handsome and brave General Gist of South Carolina. I loved General Gist, and when I mention his name tears gather in my eyes."[7]

One post-war yarn told by a "Colonel Anderson" of the U.S. Army falls in a category by itself. In this fanciful tale Gist is killed as his mount leaps airborne over the Federal works, and is then buried by the Union army with military honors![8]

Appendix Two
The Staff of States Rights Gist Brigadier General Provisional Army of the Confederate States

Dates indicate when duties were assumed; rank is the highest attained in that position.[1]

Bowie, J.A., Captain, Acting Brigade Commissary.

Butler, Lee M., 2nd Lieutenant, Acting Ordnance Officer, September 1862; 1st Lieutenant, Aide-de-Camp, January 6, 1863. From Florida, Butler served as ordnance officer on the staff of Brigadier General William D. Smith before joining Gist.

Cooper, William, Major, Surgeon, September 30, 1863. Dr. Cooper was a Mississippian and worked before the war in Nashville General Hospital.

Dearing, A.J., Major, Commissary, January 6, 1863.

Dunovant, John, Captain, Aide-de-Camp, January 6, 1863.

Garden, Henry DeSaussure, Captain, Assistant Inspector General, March 10, 1864. A graduate of the South Carolina Military Academy (Citadel) class of 1859, Garden was living in Texas on the eve of the war. His brother wrote James Chesnut, Jr., asking the Senator's help in obtaining a commission for young Henry.

154

Gist, James D., Captain, Aide-de-Camp, April 22, 1862. Died at Morton, Mississippi of typhoid fever on August 24, 1863.

Glover, Joseph, Captain, Aide-de-Camp, January 6, 1863.

Green, John S., Major, Quartermaster, January 6, 1863.

Habersham, Joseph Clay, 1st Lieutenant, Aide-de-Camp, 1863. Killed at the Battle of Atlanta, July 22, 1864. Habersham was a Georgian, originally on the staff of Brigadier General William D. Smith.

Hunt, J.M., 2nd Lieutenant, Acting Ordnance Officer, September 20, 1863; 1st Lieutenant, Ordnance Officer, 1864.

King, Mallory P., Captain, Assistant Adjutant General, 1862. Formerly on Brigadier General William D. Smith's staff, after leaving Gist in July 1864 King served on the staff of Major General LaFayette McLaws.

McKinzie, W.G., Major, Surgeon, February 1864.

Nance, William F., Captain, Assistant Adjutant General, August 11, 1862. In late 1864 Nance was on the staff of Brigadier General Roswell S. Ripley.

Smith, B.B., Major, Brigade Inspector, 1863; Assistant Adjutant General, 1864. After Gist's death Smith commanded the brigade at Franklin until he was himself wounded. Smith ended the war as commander of the consolidated 16th and 24th South Carolina regiments.

Smith, R.B., Major, Acting Assistant Adjutant General, January 1863.

Tracy, Carlos, Captain, Aide-de-Camp, May 20, 1862. Before the war Tracy was in the South Carolina General Assembly. After only a few months with Gist he joined the staff of Brigadier General Johnson Hagood.

Trenholm, Frank H., 2nd Lieutenant, Aide-de-Camp, 1864.

Walker, Joseph, Captain, Assistant Adjutant General, May 1, 1862. Like Tracy, in the summer of 1862 he joined the staff of Brigadier General Johnson Hagood.

Notes to Chapter One

1. Wilson Gee, *The Gist Family of South Carolina and its Maryland Antecedents* (Charlottesville, Virginia: Jarman's, Inc., 1934), p. 44n.

2. Ibid., p. 21.

3. Ibid., pp. 3-7.

4. Allen Johnson and Dumas Malone, eds., *Dictionary of American Biography* (New York: Charles Scribner's Sons, 1960), s.v. "Christopher Gist;" Douglas Southall Freeman, *Washington,* abridgment by Richard Harwell (New York: Charles Scribner's Sons, 1968), p. 37.

5. Jean Muir Dorsey and Maxwell Jay Dorsey, *Christopher Gist of Maryland and Some of His Descendants* (Chicago: John S. Swift Co., 1958), p. 33.

6. Ibid., p. 111.

7. Johnson and Malone, *Dictionary,* s.v. "Mordecai Gist."

8. Gee, *Gist Family,* p. 18; Dorsey and Dorsey, *Christopher Gist,* pp. 111-112.

9. Ibid., pp. 112-113.

10. Gee, *Gist Family,* pp. 34-36; Margaret Adams Gist, ed., *Presbyterian Women of South Carolina* (Women's Auxiliary of the Synod of S.C., 1929), p. 403.

11. Case no. 333, October 1815, Union District Court of General Sessions, S.C. Department of Archives and History.

12. Case no. 292, October 1817, Union District Court of General Sessions, S.C. Department of Archives and History.

13. Gee, *Gist Family,* p. 37n; Thomas Campbell, *The Poetical Works* (London: Edward Moxon, 1837), p. 116.

14. In the opinion of the present owner the finely detailed house may have been built prior to Nathaniel Gist's purchase of the land. See Dorsey and Dorsey, *Christopher Gist,* p. 112.

15. Gee, *Gist Family,* pp. 37-40.

16. Robert Mills, *Statistics of South Carolina* (Charleston: Hurlbut and Lloyd, 1826), pp. 757-758; Will C. Lake, *Union County, Places and People* (Union, S.C.: Privately Printed, 1982), p. 6; Mannie Lee Mabry, ed., *Union County Heritage* (Winston-Salem, N.C.: Hunter Publishing Co., 1981), p. 338.

17. Alexander Hamilton, "The Federalist No. 85," in *The Federalist,* ed., Benjamin Fletcher Wright (Cambridge, Mass.: The Belknap Press of Harvard University Press, 1966), p. 545.

18. Alexander Stephens, *A Constitutional View of the Late War Between the States,* 2 vols. (Philadelphia: National Publishing Company, 1868), vol. 1, pp. 125 and 532.

19. *Charleston Mercury,* 3 September 1831.

20. *Mercury,* 8 September 1831 and 8 October 1831.

21. Gee, *Gist Family,* pp. 37ff. First-born of the Gist children, Louisa, died in infancy.

22. Ibid., pp. 34-35.

23. Nathaniel Gist to James H. Saye, 6 October 1839 (Papers of James Hodge Saye, South Caroliniana Library); "Notes on Saye's Academy," undated manuscript (Papers of Margaret Adams Gist, South Caroliniana Library); Ann H. Eison, "States Rights Gist," *Charleston News and Courier,* 9 July 1922, part 2, p. 17; Lousarah Belle Free, "Education in Union County, S.C. Prior to 1860" (Master's thesis, University of South Carolina, 1929), pp. 40-41; Mabry, *Heritage,* pp. 84, 172, 337-338.

24. Gee, *Gist Family,* p. 82.

Notes to Chapter Two

1. Fitz Hugh McMaster, *History of Fairfield County* (Columbia: State Commercial Printing Co., 1946), pp. 38, 60-62, 103; William Watts Ball, *The State That Forgot: South Carolina's Surrender to Democracy* (Indianapolis: Bobbs-Merrill Co., 1932), p. 51; William P. Dubose, "Recollections of Mt. Zion School," *The Educational*, January 1903, pp. 256-260; B.J. Wells, "Sketch of James·Hudson," c. 1900 (Papers of James Wilson Hudson, South Caroliniana Library).

2. Daniel Walker Hollis, *The University of South Carolina,* 2 vols. (Columbia: University of South Carolina Press, 1951), vol. 1: *South Carolina College,* pp. 136, 149-150; Maximilian LaBorde, *History of South Carolina College* (Charleston: Walker, Evans and Cogswell, 1874), p. 277.

3. Hollis, *College,* pp. 178-183.

4. Ibid., pp. 95-96, 104-105.

5. Ibid., pp. 161, 164-166.

6. Margaret L. Coit, *John C. Calhoun: American Portrait* (Boston: Houghton Mifflin Co., 1950), p. 285.

7. Otto J. Scott, *The Secret Six: John Brown and the Abolitionist Movement* (New York: Time Books, 1979), p. 93.

8. William Harper, et. al., *The Pro-Slavery Argument* (Philadelphia: Lippincott, Grambo & Co., 1853), p. 6; Alexis de Tocqueville, *Democracy in America,* ed., J.P. Mayer, trans., George Lawrence (Garden City, N.Y.: Doubleday, 1969), p. 343.

9. Hollis, *College,* pp. 232-246, passim; *Catalogue of the Regular and Honorary Members of the Clariosophic Society of the South Carolina College* (Columbia: R.W. Gibbes, 1853), pp. 38, 49.

10. *Catalogue of the Trustees, Faculty and Students of the South Carolina College* (Columbia: I.C. Morgan, 1848), p. 12; *Catalogue of the Trustees, Faculty and Students of the South Carolina College* (Columbia: A.S. Johnson, 1849), p. 10.

11. *College Catalogue,* 1848, p. 16; *College Catalogue,* 1849, p. 16; *Catalogue of the Trustees, Faculty and Students of the South Carolina College* (Columbia: A.S. Johnson, 1851), p. 19.

12. *College Catalogue,* 1851, p. 6; South Carolina College Diploma of States Rights Gist, 2 December 1850 (Papers of States Rights Gist, South Caroliniana Library); *Charleston Courier,* 4 December 1850; *Mercury,* 4 December 1850.

13. Palmetto State disunionism at mid-century is concisely treated in Philip M. Hamer, *The Secession Movement in South Carolina, 1847-1852* (New York: DaCapo Press, 1971).

14. David E. Finley, manuscript dated December 1906 (Papers of David E. Finley, South Caroliniana Library). A Gist family member, while a student Finley wrote this brief sketch of the life of States Rights Gist. It is valuable for details he could only have learned from those close to the General.

15. Charles Warren, *History of the Harvard Law School* (New York: DaCapo Press, 1970), vol. 2, pp. 91 and 337.

16. Samuel Eliot Morison, *Three Centuries of Harvard: 1636-1936* (Cambridge, Mass.: The Belknap Press of Harvard University Press, 1936), pp. 238 and 240; Warren, *Law School,* pp. 184-185; *The Centennial History of the Harvard Law School, 1817-1917* (n.p.: Harvard Law School Association, 1918), pp. 379 and 396.

17. Warren, *Law School,* p. 156.

18. Ibid., pp. 159-160.

19. Morison, *Three Centuries,* p. 290.

20. Ibid., p. 303; *Centennial History,* pp. 398-399.

21. Ibid., p. 20; Warren, *Law School,* p. 345; *Centennial History,* pp. 78-79.

22. Warren, *Law School,* p. 305.

23. Samuel A. Eliot, *A Sketch of the History of Harvard College and Its Present State* (Boston: Charles C. Little and James Brown, 1848), pp. 122-123; Warren, *Law School,* pp. 175-176.

24. Ibid., p. 194.

25. Hollis, *College*, pp. 163 and 167; B.M. Palmer, *The Life and Letters of James Henley Thornwell, DD, LLD* (Richmond: Whittet and Shepperson, 1875), p. 363.

26. Gee, *Gist Family*, p. 37. The real-life "Gertrude of Wyoming" proudly recounted the unlikely story behind her name until her death in 1928.

27. Harvard Law School Certificate of States Rights Gist, 1 October 1852 (Papers of States Rights Gist, South Caroliniana Library).

28. Ibid.; Warren *Law School*, vol. 3, p. 57; *Quinquennial Catalog of the Law School of Harvard University, 1817-1934* (Cambridge, Mass.: Published by the Law School, 1935), p. 44. The evidence clearly disproves family tradition that Gist completed the course and graduated from Harvard Law School.

29. Jack K. Williams, "The Criminal Lawyer in Antebellum South Carolina," in *The Legal Profession: Major Historical Interpretations,* ed., Kermit L. Hall (New York: Garland Publishing, 1987), p. 647; States Rights Gist's Certificate of Admission to the South Carolina Bar, 10 May 1853 (Papers of States Rights Gist, South Caroliniana Library).

30. *Unionville Journal,* 19 July 1854 and many other issues in 1854 and 1855. At one time or another States Rights Gist would form partnerships with brother James, William Munro and "R.J. Gist" (possibly brother Robert T. Gist). See Estate Papers of States Rights Gist, Box 47, Package 4, 1865 (Union County Probate Court Records, South Carolina Department of Archives and History).

31. Ibid.; B.F. Arthur, Jr., "Random Notes: Arthur History," 28 May 1942 manuscript (Papers of Benjamin Franklin Arthur, South Caroliniana Library); *Journal,* 9 March 1855; Williams, "Criminal Lawyer," pp. 642-652, passim.

Notes to Chapter Three

1. *The Uniform of the Militia of South Carolina as Prescribed by the General Assembly at its Session of 1839* (Columbia: A.H. Pemberton, 1840), p. 9; *The Militia and Patrol Laws of South Carolina: To December, 1851* (Columbia: Johnson and Cavis, 1852), p. 3; Eison, "States Rights Gist;" *Miller's Planters' and Merchants' Almanac* (Charleston: 1853).

2. Spartanburg *Carolina Spartan,* 10 September 1857; *Courier,* 30 December 1864.

3. *Militia Laws, 1851,* pp. 3-38, passim.

4. *Journal,* 28 July 1854.

5. J.F. Williams, *Old and New Columbia* (Columbia: Epworth Orphanage Press, 1929), pp. 44-45. For an insightful and amusing discussion of the militia see James J. Pettigrew, "The Militia System of South Carolina," *Russell's Magazine,* March 1860, pp. 529-540.

6. Augustus Dickert, *History of Kershaw's Brigade* (Newberry, S.C.: Elbert H. Aull, Co., 1899), pp. 15-16.

7. Ibid.

8. *Yorkville Enquirer,* 30 August 1855.

9. *Minutes of the Military Commission at the Meeting in Greenville, S.C., August 4th 1859* (Charleston: Evans and Co., 1859), pp. 10-12.

10. *Journal,* 3 August 1855.

11. *Courier,* 30 December 1864.

12. Ibid.; "Brigadier General States Rights Gist," undated manuscript (Papers of Margaret Adams Gist, South Caroliniana Library). States

Rights Gist was "orator" at the Unionville Female Academy's "May Party" in 1855. See Allan D. Charles, *The Narrative History of Union County, S.C.* (Spartanburg, S.C.: The Reprint Co., 1987), p. 127.

13. *Spartan,* 21 December 1854.

14. *Enquirer,* 13 March 1856, 24 January 1856 and 8 May 1856; *Spartan,* 8 May 1856.

15. *Spartan,* 5 June 1856.

16. *Spartan,* 7 August 1856 and 21 August 1856.

17. *Enquirer,* 21 August 1856.

18. *Spartan,* 14 August 1856 and 30 July 1857.

19. *Enquirer,* 19 August 1858. Melton held the rank of major. Previously he was editor of the *Chester Standard,* a paper unrestrained in its criticism of the militia system. See *Spartan,* 26 August 1858 and *Chester Standard,* 11 September 1856.

20. *Spartan,* 10 September 1857.

21. *Journal,* 27 August 1858; *Enquirer,* 8 September 1859.

Notes to Chapter Four

1. Johnson and Malone, *Dictionary,* s.v. "William Henry Gist;" Daniel J. Bell, "Interpretive Booklets for Local Historic Sites: Rose Hill State Park, Union, S.C. as a Model" (Master's thesis, University of South Carolina, 1983), pp. 16-17, 19, 24-26 and 33-34.

2. Stephen B. Oates, *To Purge This Land With Blood: A Biography of John Brown* (Amherst: University of Massachusetts Press, 1984), pp. 30, 134-137 and 292-301; Scott, *Secret Six,* pp. 299 and 303. Examples of the eulogies to Brown can be found in Louis Ruchames, ed., *A John Brown Reader* (London: Abelard-Schuman, 1959).

3. *Enquirer,* 8 September 1859.

4. *Enquirer,* 23 December 1858; W.H. Gist to B.T. Watts, 5 September 1859 and W.H. Gist to B.T. Watts, 6 May 1860 (Papers of Beaufort T. Watts, South Caroliniana Library).

5. *Spartan,* 12 April 1860.

6. For Governor Gist's letter and the replies see John G. Nicolay and John Hay, *Abraham Lincoln: A History* (New York: The Century Co., 1917), vol. 2, pp. 306-314.

7. B.T. Watts to General Hammond, n.d. (Papers of Beaufort T. Watts, South Caroliniana Library). States Rights Gist was in Unionville on 18 October 1860 long enough to make a bill with a local merchant (see S.R. Gist estate papers). Either he stopped at Unionville briefly after returning from North Carolina or Governor Ellis received his letter in the mail. The governors of North Carolina and Louisiana do not mention courier Gist, leaving it an open question whether he visited these states. Governor Gist's letter to Governor Ellis is in the John W. Ellis Papers, Southern Historical Collection.

8. *Journal of the Senate of South Carolina Being the Annual Session of 1860* (Columbia: R.W. Gibbes, 1860), p. 23; *Journal of the House of*

Representatives of the State of South Carolina Being the Sessions of 1860 (Columbia: R.W. Gibbes, 1860), pp. 13 and 26. The day after Lincoln's election the "Newman Guards," a Georgia militia unit, offered their services to Governor Gist in support of South Carolina's expected secession. States Rights Gist replied that the Governor "hopes soon to see your gallant state side by side with South Carolina, battling for the rights of the South." States Rights Gist to George M. Hanvey, 12 November 1860 (George M. Hanvey Papers, Southern Historical Collection).

9. *Senate Journal 1860,* p. 68.

10. Lillian Adele Kibler, *Benjamin F. Perry: South Carolina Unionist* (Durham, N.C.: Duke University Press, 1946), p. 348; *Courier,* 30 December 1864. Perry expressed his supreme loyalty to South Carolina in 1830 and never wavered thereafter.

Notes to Chapter Five

1. Sub-committee of the 1860 Association, G. Manigault, Chairman, *Suggestions As to the Arming of the State* (Charleston: Evans and Cogswell, 1860), pp. 4-5.

2. *Statutes at Large of South Carolina* (Columbia: Republican Printing Co., 1874), vol. 12, pp. 726-730; Charles E. Cauthen, *South Carolina Goes to War 1860-1865,* (Chapel Hill, N.C.: University of North Carolina Press, 1950), pp. 113-114.

3. Ibid.; *Journal of the Convention of the People of South Carolina* (Charleston: Evans and Cogswell, 1861), pp. 159-160.

4. *Statutes,* pp. 730-732; Cauthen, *War,* p. 115.

5. *Statutes,* pp. 732-734; William James Rivers, *Rivers' Account of the Raising of Troops in South Carolina for State and Confederate Service 1861-1865* (Columbia: Bryan Printing, 1899), p. 6.

6. *Enquirer,* 10 January 1861; Rivers, *Account,* pp. 7, 8 and 10.

7. *Militia Laws 1851,* p. 14; *Statutes,* p. 732.

8. Rivers, *Account,* pp. 7 and 9; *Mercury,* 17 January 1861; *Enquirer,* 7 February 1861. Early January issues of the *Mercury* refer to Gist as "Acting Adjutant and Inspector General;" by January 17 "Acting" was dropped. Pickens sent a message to the General Assembly on 27 January 1861 asking for the election of an Adjutant and Inspector General, but the lawmakers were in a hurry to adjourn and did so without making a choice. The Convention had expanded on 27 December 1860 the Governor's power to appoint officers "whose appointment otherwise shall not have been provided for by law." Pickens may have concluded that the Convention's ambiguous language implied sufficient authority for him to fill this vacancy. *Mercury,* 30 January 1861 and 28 December 1860.

9. Charles E. Cauthen, ed., *Journals of the South Carolina Executive Councils of 1861 and 1862* (Columbia: Archives Department, 1956), pp. 36 and 37.

10. William Howard Russell, *My Diary North and South* (Boston: T.O. Burnham, 1863), p. 121; Captain of Engineers to States Rights Gist, 24 January 1861; Walter Gwynn to States Rights Gist, 1 February 1861; Walter Gwynn to States Rights Gist, 2 February 1861 (S.C. Engineer Bureau Records, South Caroliniana Library).

11. States Rights Gist to R.G.M. Dunovant, 9 February 1861, 22 February 1861 and 24 February 1861 (R.G.M. Dunovant Papers, Duke University); E. Milby Burton, *The Siege of Charleston 1861-1865* (Columbia: University of South Carolina Press, 1970), p. 28.

12. Alfred Roman, *The Military Operations of General Beauregard* (New York: Harper Brothers, 1884), p. 41; W.A. Harris, compiler, *The Record of Fort Sumter From Its Occupation By Major Anderson to Its Reduction by South Carolina Troops* (Columbia: S.C. Steam Job Printing Office, 1862), p. 48; U.S. War Department, compiler, *War of the Rebellion: A Compilation of the Official Records of the Union and Confederate Armies* (Washington: Government Printing Office, 1880-1901), ser. 1, vol. 1, p 34.

13. Charles W. Ramsdell, "Lincoln and Fort Sumter," *The Journal of Southern History,* August 1937, pp. 280-282; John Shipley Tilley, *Lincoln Takes Command* (Chapel Hill, N.C.: University of North Carolina Press, 1941), pp. 263-264.

14. States Rights Gist to Joseph B. Kershaw, 6 April 1861 and 8 April 1861 (Papers of Joseph Brevard Kershaw, South Caroliniana Library); Cauthen, *War,* p. 130n.

15. Tilley, *Lincoln,* pp. 266-267.

16. Russell, *Diary,* pp. 105-106.

Notes to Chapter Six

1. W.H. Gist to B.T. Watts, 17 May 1861 (Papers of Beaufort T. Watts, South Caroliniana Library).

2. States Rights Gist to Joseph B. Kershaw, 16 April 1861 and 20 April 1861 (Papers of Joseph Brevard Kershaw, South Caroliniana Library); Thomas B. Walsh to States Rights Gist, 21 May 1861 (Papers of Thomas B. Walsh, South Caroliniana Library).

3. States Rights Gist to James Simons, 27 May 1861 and Francis W. Pickens to James Simons, 6 July 1861 (Papers of James Simons, South Caroliniana Library). The controversy is documented in the South Caroliniana Library's Gist-Simons correspondence and in James Simons, *Address to the Officers of the Fourth Brigade Giving the Grounds of His Resignation* (Charleston: Evans and Cogswell, 1861).

4. *O.R.*, ser. 2, vol. 3, p. 4; Howard P. Nash, Jr., *A Naval History of the Civil War* (New York: A.S. Barnes, 1972), pp. 294-295.

5. *O.R.*, ser. 4, vol. 1, pp. 420-421.

6. *O.R.*, ser. 4, vol. 1, p. 480; *O.R.*, ser. 1, vol. 2, p. 973.

7. *O.R.*, ser. 1, vol. 2, p. 492.

8. Ibid.; Robert Underwood and Clarence Clough Buel, eds., *Battles and Leaders of the Civil War* (New York: The Century Co., 1884-1887), vol. 1, p. 210.

9. Clement A. Evans, ed., *Confederate Military History*, (Atlanta: Confederate Publishing, 1899), vol. 5: *South Carolina*, p. 26.

10. Douglas Southall Freeman, *Lee's Lieutenants: A Study in Command* (New York: Charles Scribner's Sons, 1942), vol. 1, p. 72.

11. Mary Chesnut, *The Private Mary Chesnut: The Unpublished Civil War Diaries,* ed., C. Vann Woodward (New York: Oxford University Press, 1984), p. 132; Mary Chesnut, *Mary Chesnut's Civil War,* ed., C. Vann Woodward (New Haven: Yale University Press, 1981), p. 153.

12. *O.R.,* ser. 4, vol. 1, p. 582.

13. *O.R.,* ser. 4, vol. 1, pp. 614 and 615; *O.R.,* ser. 1, vol. 6, p. 273.

14. Ibid., p. 335.

15. Ibid., pp. 336 and 345; *O.R.,* ser. 1, vol. 53, pp. 198-199.

16. *Journal of the Senate of South Carolina Being the Sessions of 1861* (Columbia: Charles P. Pelham, 1861), p. 60.

17. Gee, *Gist Family,* pp. 31-32.

18. Chesnut, *Civil War,* p. 265.

19. *O.R.,* ser. 4, vol. 1, p. 614; Cauthen *War,* pp. 142-145.

20. James Chesnut, Jr., *Report of the Chief of the Department of the Military of South Carolina to His Excellency Governor Pickens* (Columbia: Charles P. Pelham, 1862), p. 5.

21. Walter B. Capers, *The Soldier-Bishop: Ellison Capers* (New York: Neale Publishing Co., 1912), p. 51; Cauthen, *Journals,* p. 95.

22. Chesnut, *Report,* pp. 6-7; *O.R.,* ser. 4, vol. 1, pp. 975-976; Cauthen, *Journals,* pp. 102-103, 107, 110, 113 and 123; *O.R.,* ser. 4, vol. 1, pp. 976-977; States Rights Gist to William Porcher Miles, telegram dated 17 March 1862 (William Porcher Miles Papers, Southern Historical Collection).

23. Chesnut, *Report,* p. 7; Cauthen, *War,* p. 177n.

24. Kibler, *Perry,* p. 360.

25. Cauthen, *Journals,* pp. 173-174; James Chesnut, Jr. to William Porcher Miles, 14 March 1862 (William Porcher Miles Papers, Southern Historical Collection); *Journal of the Congress of the Confederate States of America, 1861-1865* (Washington: Government Printing Office, 1904), vol. 2, pp. 78-81.

26. Chesnut, *Civil War,* p. 320.

27. Gee, *Gist Family,* p. 87.

28. *O.R.,* ser. 1, vol. 6, p. 430; States Rights Gist to William Porcher Miles, two telegrams dated 1 April 1862 (William Porcher Miles Papers, Southern Historical Collection).

29. *Mercury,* 25 March 1862.

Notes to Chapter Seven

1. Laura J. Hopkins, *Lower Richland Planters: Hopkins, Adams, Weston and Related Families of South Carolina* (Columbia: Privately Printed by R.L. Bryan Co., 1976), p. 346.

2. Johnson and Malone, *Dictionary,* s.v. "James Hopkins Adams;" Gee, *Gist Family,* p. 38. Many of Governor Adams' views were thought radical even by South Carolina standards. Most balked when he advocated a re-opening of the slave trade. As a member of the Secession Convention he voted against adoption of the Confederate Constitution, presumably because that document outlawed the slave trade and permitted future admission of non-slaveholding states.

3. Margaret Simons Middleton, *Live Oak Plantation, Congaree, South Carolina* (Charleston: Nelson Printing Co., 1956), pp. 8-9; *Courier,* 30 December 1864.

4. See Appendix 2.

5. *O.R.,* ser. 1, vol. 14, p. 476.

6. Cauthen, *Journals,* pp. 173-174; *O.R.,* ser. 4, vol. 1, pp. 1106-1107; John P. Thomas, *History of the South Carolina Military Academy* (Charleston: Walker, Evans and Cogswell, 1893), pp. 182-188. Ironically, Gist had written Congressman Miles some months before, praising Jones as "decidedly the best military man in the State, without any regular military education." States Rights Gist to William Porcher Miles, 12 December 1861 (William Porcher Miles Papers, Southern Historical Collection).

7. *O.R.,* ser. 1, vol. 14, pp. 476, 499-502.

8. Ibid., pp. 493, 499-500, 520 and 529; Burton, *Siege,* p. 99.

9. Ibid., pp. 92-93.

10. Ibid., pp. 92 and 97-98; Evans, ed., *History*, vol. 5: *South Carolina*, p. 80.

11. *O.R.*, ser. 1, vol. 14, pp. 16 and 18-19; "Memoir of the Marion Rifles," n.d. (John Henry Steinmeyer, Jr. Papers, Southern Historical Collection).

12. Burton, *Siege*, p. 99.

13. *O.R.*, ser. 1, vol. 14, pp. 534-537; [Carlos Tracy], "A Rebel Soldier's Diary of the Enemy's Approach to and Withdrawal from Before Charleston, S.C., May, June and July, 1862," in *Rebellion Record*, ed., Frank Moore (New York: G.P. Putnam, 1862-1871), vol. 5, pp. 279-280.

14. Ibid.; Johnson Hagood, *Memoirs of the War of Secession* (Columbia: The State Co., 1910), pp. 90-91 and 93-94.

15. *O.R.*, ser. 1, vol. 14, p. 91.

16. Hagood, *Memoirs*, pp. 93 and 97; Ellison Capers to his wife, 17 June 1862 (Ellison Capers Collection, Citadel Archives). Evans himself was anything but coy. Author of a letter published in the *Mercury* June 23, the General insisted that he "commanded in person the engagement" and therefore could not be denied a share of the glory.

17. *O.R.*, ser. 1, vol. 14, pp. 568, 571 and 581-582.

18. Ibid., pp. 578, 580 and 581.

19. Ibid., pp. 585 and 591.

20. Ibid., pp. 619-625.

21. *Mercury*, 11 October 1862 and 13 October 1862.

22. *O.R.*, ser. 1, vol. 14, pp. 639 and 651; Roman, *Beauregard*, vol. 2, p. 32.

23. Cauthen, *Journals*, pp. 270 and 276.

24. *O.R.*, ser. 1, vol. 14, pp. 616, 631 and 641.

25. Ibid., pp. 652-656; Roman, *Beauregard*, vol. 2 pp. 33-34.

26. *O.R.*, ser. 1, vol. 14, pp. 713-715.

27. Ibid., p. 739.

28. Ibid., pp. 741-742.

29. *O.R.,* ser. 1, vol. 18, pp. 827-830.

30. General Order No. 1 dated 6 January 1863, Inspection Report dated 11 January 1863, General Order No. 2 dated 12 January 1863 and States Rights Gist to General Clingman, 16 January 1863 (Thomas L. Clingman Papers, Southern Historical Collection).

31. *O.R.,* ser. 1, vol. 18, pp. 836 and 837; *O.R.,* ser. 1, vol. 14, p. 776.

32. *O.R.,* ser. 1, vol. 18, p. 867; *O.R.,* ser. 1, vol. 14, pp. 804-807.

33. Ibid., pp. 764 and 807.

34. Ibid., pp. 812-813.

35. Ibid., p. 815.

36. Ibid., pp. 829-833.

37. Ibid., p. 277; Roman, *Beauregard,* vol. 2, p. 70.

38. Theodore A. Honour to Beckie Honour, 24 April 1863 (Papers of Theodore A. Honour, South Caroliniana Library); Hagood, *Memoirs,* p. 112.

39. Susan Middleton to Harriott Middleton, *South Carolina Historical and Genealogical Magazine,* April 1963, p. 97; Theodore Honour to Beckie Honour, 24 April 1863 (Papers of Theodore A. Honour, South Caroliniana Library). Susan Middleton dismissed the General as a "greenhorn and nonentity." The demoralized Honour found little in army life to his liking and continually threatened to "run the blockade" (desert). He claimed that Gist "is a man that we place very little confidence in as a General."

40. Personal Journal of Ellison Capers, 23 April 1863 (Ellison Capers Collection, Citadel Archives); *O.R.,* ser. 1, vol. 14, p. 918; Hagood, *Memoirs,* p. 112.

41. Theodore A. Honour to Beckie Honour, 21 April 1863 (Papers of Theodore A. Honour, South Caroliniana Library).

Notes to Chapter Eight

1. *O.R.,* ser. 1, vol. 14, pp. 923, 925 and 931.

2. Ibid., pp. 925 and 926; *O.R.,* ser. 1, vol. 24, part 3, pp. 833 and 862.

3. Ibid., p. 833; Ellison Capers to his wife, 8 May 1863 (Ellison Capers Collection, Citadel Archives).

4. David E. Finley, manuscript dated December 1906 (Papers of David E. Finley, South Caroliniana Library); Hopkins, *Lower Richland Planters,* pp. 339-358; Middleton, *Live Oak,* p. 5.

5. Capers, *Soldier-Bishop,* p. 61; Ellison Capers to his wife, 12 May 1863 (Ellison Capers Collection, Citadel Archives).

6. Ellison Capers to his wife, 8 May 1863 (Ellison Capers Collection. Citadel Archives); "Memoirs of the Marion Rifles," n.d. (John Henry Steinmeyer, Jr. Papers, Southern Historical Collection).

7. *O.R.,* ser. 1, vol. 24, part 3, p. 862; Evans, ed., *History.* vol. 5: *South Carolina,* p. 204.

8. *O.R.,* ser. 1, vol. 24, part 1, p. 787.

9. *O.R.,* ser. 1, vol. 24, part 3, pp. 883-884.

10. Ibid., pp. 886-887, 889, 897, and 920.

11. Ibid., p. 920.

12. Ibid.; *O.R.,* ser. 1, vol. 24, part 2, p. 426; Evans, ed., *History.* vol. 6: *Georgia,* pp. 449-451; Ezra J. Warner, *Generals in Gray* (Baton Rouge: Louisiana State University Press, 1959), s.v. "William Henry Talbot Walker;" *O.R.,* ser. 1, vol. 24, part 3, pp. 925-926.

13. Evans, ed., *History,* vol. 5: *South Carolina,* p. 211.

14. Ibid., p. 212; Gee, *Gist Family*, pp. 90-93; James D. Gist file, "Compiled Service Records of Confederate General and Staff Officers, and Non-Regimental Enlisted Men," U.S. National Archives.

15. Evans, ed., *History*, vol. 5: *South Carolina*, p. 277.

16. Personal Journal of Ellison Capers, 13 September 1863 (Ellison Capers Collection, Citadel Archives); Ellison Capers to his wife, 13 September 1863 (Ellison Capers Papers, Duke University).

Notes to Chapter Nine

1. Glenn Tucker, *Chickamauga: Bloody Battle in the West* (Indianapolis: Bobbs-Merrill, 1961), p. 219.

2. *O.R.,* ser. 1, vol. 30, part 2, p. 244; C.I. Walker, "Historical Address," *Ceremonies at the Unveiling of the South Carolina Monument on the Chickamauga Battlefield May 27th, 1901* (n.p., n.d.), pp. 13-14.

3. *O.R.,* ser. 1, vol. 30, part 2, p. 245; Capers, *Soldier-Bishop,* p. 68.

4. Ibid., pp. 68-71; *O.R.,* ser. 1, vol. 30, part 2, pp. 245-246.

5. Tucker, *Chickamauga,* p. 364. According to Tucker, General Turchin believed the Federal army would probably have been destroyed had the Confederate advance "been combined with flank and rear attacks by Liddell's division supported by Gist..."

6. *O.R.,* ser. 1, vol. 30, part 2, p. 246.

7. Ibid., p. 243.

8. Gee, *Gist Family,* p. 42.

9. *O.R.,* ser. 1, vol. 30, part 2, p. 242; "Memoir of the Marion Rifles," n.d. (John Henry Steinmeyer, Jr. Papers, Southern Historical Collection).

10. *O.R.,* ser. 1, vol. 30, part 4, pp. 734-736.

11. Hudson Strode, *Jefferson Davis: Confederate President* (New York: Harcourt, Brace and World, 1959), p. 481.

12. James Cooper Nisbet, *Four Years on the Firing Line,* ed., Bell Irvin Wiley (Jackson, Tennessee: McCowat-Mercer Press, 1963), pp. 156-157.

13. Ibid., p. 141; *O.R.*, ser. 1, vol. 31, part 2, pp. 685-686, 702 and 717-718.

14. Nisbet, *Firing Line*, p. 153.

15. *O.R.*, ser. 1, vol. 31, part 2, pp. 718, 722 and 734.

16. Nisbet, *Firing Line*, pp. 156-158.

17. *O.R.*, ser. 1, vol. 31, part 2, pp. 751-752.

18. Nisbet, *Firing Line*, pp. 157-158; J.H. Steinmeyer to Ellison Capers, 9 November 1877 and 6 June 1900 (Ellison Capers Papers, Duke University); "Memoir of the Marion Rifles," n.d. (John Henry Steinmeyer, Jr. Papers, Southern Historical Collection).

19. William C. Davis, *Breckinridge: Statesman, Soldier, Symbol* (Baton Rouge: Louisiana State University Press, 1974), p. 390.

20. *O.R.*, ser. 1, vol. 31, part 2, p. 752; Nisbet, *Firing Line*, pp. 160-161.

21. *O.R.*, ser. 1, vol. 31, part 2, pp. 96 and 752. Nisbet, *Firing Line*, pp. 160-161.

22. Ibid., pp. 161-164.

23. Ibid.

24. Ibid., p. 165.

25. Ibid.; James Lee McDonough, *Chattanooga: A Death Grip on the Confederacy* (Knoxville: University of Tennessee Press, 1984), pp. 220-225.

26. William H.T. Walker to Mary Walker, 3 December 1863 (William H.T. Walker Papers, Duke University).

27. William M. Polk, *Leonidas Polk: Bishop and General* (New York: Longmans, Green and Co., 1915), p. 313; Davis, *Breckinridge*, pp. 396-399.

28. *O.R.*, ser. 1, vol. 31, part 2, p. 666.

Notes to Chapter Ten

1. William H.T. Walker to Mary Walker, 11 December 1863 (William H.T. Walker Papers, Duke University); Richard Irvine Manning to his mother, 28 January 1864 (Richard Irvine Manning Papers, South Caroliniana Library); *Charleston Daily Courier,* 31 March 1864; Columbia *Daily South Carolinian,* 6 May 1864; *O.R.,* ser. 1, vol. 38, part 3, p. 713.

2. *O.R.,* ser. 1, vol. 32, part 2, p. 708; Letter of Clement Hoffman Stevens, 19 April 1864 (Clement Hoffman Stevens Papers, South Caroliniana Library).

3. Freeman, *Lee's Lieutenants,* vol. 3, p. xx.

4. *O.R.,* ser. 1, vol. 52, part 2, pp. 628 and 629; *Journal of Confederate Congress,* vol. 4, pp. 19 and 31.

5. Robert M. McBride and Dan M. Robinson, *Biographical Directory of the Tennessee General Assembly* (Nashville: Tennessee Historical Commission, 1975), vol. 1, pp. 337-338. Governor Harris was not adverse to using his influence on military appointments. As far back as 1861 the Governor scolded President Davis for not consulting him before appointing Tennesseans general officers. See *O.R.,* ser. 4, vol. 1, pp. 474-475 and 480; Dunbar Rowland, ed., *Jefferson Davis, Constitutionalist: His Letters, Papers and Speeches* (Jackson, Miss.: Miss. Department of Archives and History, 1923), vol. 6, pp. 49-50 and vol. 5, p. 595; *O.R.,* ser. 1, vol. 32, part 2, p. 806.

6. *O.R.,* ser. 1, vol. 52, part 3, pp. 586-592; Howell and Elizabeth Purdue, *Pat Cleburne: Confederate General* (Hillsboro, Texas: Hill Junior College Press, 1973), pp. 268-278; Thomas L. Connelly, *Autumn of Glory: The Army of Tennessee, 1862-1865* (Baton Rouge: Louisiana State University Press, 1971), pp. 318-321; Steven E. Woodworth, *Jefferson Davis and His Generals* (Lawrence, Kansas: University Press of Kansas, 1990), pp. 262-263; Christopher Losson,

Tennessee's Forgotten Warriors: Frank Cheatham and His Confederate Division (Knoxville: University of Tennessee Press, 1989), pp. 137-140.

7. Diary of George A. Mercer, vol. 2 (George A. Mercer Papers, Southern Historical Collection); *Courier,* 15 June 1864; *O.R.,* ser. 1, vol. 38, part 3, p. 713.

8. Ibid., pp. 713-714.

9. Ibid., pp. 32-33, 377, 378 and 400.

10. Ibid., pp. 704 and 714.

11. Ibid., p. 714.

12. Ibid., pp. 378 and 981.

13. Ibid., pp. 714-715; B.B. Smith to Ellison Capers, 20 July 1885 (Ellison Capers Collection, Citadel Archives).

14. *O.R.,* ser. 1, vol. 38, part 3, pp. 715-716; "Memoirs of the Marion Rifles," n.d. (John Henry Steinmeyer, Jr. Papers, Southern Historical Collection).

15. *O.R.,* ser. 1, vol. 38, part 3, p. 716.

16. Ibid.

17. Ibid.

18. Ibid.

19. Ibid., pp. 716-717.

20. Ibid.

21. Ibid., p. 717.

22. Ibid.; Ellison Capers to Joseph E. Johnston, 4 July 1874 (Ellison Capers Collection, Citadel Archives).

23. William H.T. Walker to Mary Walker, 16 July 1864 (William H.T. Walker Papers, Duke University).

24. *O.R.,* ser. 1, vol. 38, part 3, pp. 679 and 717.

25. W.T. Sherman, *Memoirs,* (New York: Charles L. Webster, 1891), vol. 2, p. 73; *O.R.,* ser. 1, vol. 38, part 3, pp. 935 and 937; *O.R.,* ser. 1, vol. 38, part 5, p. 190.

26. J.H. Steinmeyer to Ellison Capers, 18 March 1880 (Ellison Capers Papers, Duke University); Nisbet, *Firing Line,* p. 212; B.B. Smith to Ellison Capers, 3 April 1880 (Ellison Capers Collection, Citadel Archives); *O.R.,* ser. 1, vol. 38, part 5, p. 900; States Rights Gist file, "Compiled Service Records;" "States Rights Gist," *Garnet and Black* (Columbia: South Carolina College, 1902); Spencer Bidwell King, Jr., *Ebb Tide, As Seen Through the Diary of Josephine Clay Habersham, 1863* (Athens: University of Georgia Press, 1958), p. 116. General Gist's widow had a hand in writing the brief sketch for the college annual. See Janie M. Brooks to "Minnie," 10 March 1911 (Margaret Adams Gist Papers, South Caroliniana Library).

27. Sherman, *Memoirs,* vol. 2, p. 80.

28. *O.R.,* ser. 1, vol. 38, part 3, pp. 660 and 680.

29. Samuel Carter, III, *The Siege of Atlanta, 1864* (New York: St. Martin's Press, 1973), pp. 265, 267, 283-285 and 287.

30. States Rights Gist file, "Compiled Service Records;" *O.R.,* ser. 1, vol. 38, part 3, pp. 283, 708 and 728.

31. Ibid., pp. 668 and 718-720.

32. Ibid., p. 720.

33. Ibid., p. 283. General Harrow reported capture of Gist's "servant and horses, with equipments..." Either Wiley Howard was not the servant taken, or he later escaped to rejoin his master.

34. Ibid., pp. 916 and 919.

Notes to Chapter Eleven

1. *O.R.,* ser. 1, vol. 39, part 2, p. 851.

2. Capers, *Soldier-Bishop,* pp. 101-102.

3. *O.R.,* ser. 1, vol. 45, part 1, p. 733.

4. Ibid.; Sherman, *Memoirs,* p. 152.

5. Personal Journal of Ellison Capers, 9 October 1864 (Ellison Capers Collection, Citadel Archives); Pinckney Maxwell to Ellison Capers, 24 October 1864 (Ellison Capers Collection, Citadel Archives). The Ellison Capers Papers at Duke University contain a tantalizing fragment of an undated letter, possibly written by Colonel Capers late in 1864, predicting his promotion to brigadier and Gist's promotion to major general. According to the writer, "Gist has been assured by Beauregard that his assignment to S.C., in compliance with [new coastal commander] Hardee's request, will be made *after this Tenn. campaign.*" [Emphasis in the original.]

6. *O.R.,* ser. 1, vol. 45, part 1, pp. 733-734.

7. Ibid., pp. 734-735; Sherman, *Memoirs,* p. 156.

8. Ellison Capers to his wife, 14 November 1864 (Ellison Capers Papers, Duke University); *O.R.,* ser. 1, vol. 45, part 1, pp. 735-736.

9. Ibid., p. 736; Capers, *Soldier-Bishop,* p. 107.

10. Ibid., p. 106.

11. Gee, *Gist Family,* p. 84. Wiley Howard's account was recorded by the Gist family in black English. This author has made no changes except to put the words in standard English.

180

12. Ibid., p 85.

13. *O.R.,* ser. 1, vol. 45, part 1, p. 736.

14. Ibid., p. 737. Gist shouted, "Victory to the 24th!" as he passed that regiment. See Capers' account of the Tennessee campaign, n.d. (Ellison Capers Papers, Duke University).

15. Gee, *Gist Family,* pp. 85-86.

16. *O.R.,* ser. 1, vol. 45, part 1, p. 270.

17. See Appendix 1.

18. Gee, *Gist Family,* p. 86.

19. *O.R.,* ser. 1, vol. 45, part 1, p. 738; Capers' account of the Tennessee campaign, n.d. (Ellison Capers Papers, Duke University). Of Gist's staff only Captain H.D. Garden came through the battle unhurt.

20. Gee, *Gist Family,* p. 87.

21. *Courier,* 3 January 1865.

22. Chesnut, *Civil War,* p. 692.

23. *Courier,* 30 December 1864.

24. Gee, *Gist Family,* p. 87.

Notes to Epilogue

Middleton, *Live Oak,* pp. 12-13.

2. Estate Papers of States Rights Gist. Throughout life Gist would be plagued by misspellings of his name. The most common mistake changed "Rights" to "Right," an error committed by even the engraver of his cemetery monument.

3. Columbia *Daily Phoenix,* 8 May 1866; Columbia *Tri-Weekly Phoenix,* 10 May 1866.

4. Estate Papers of States Rights Gist.

5. Middleton, *Live Oak,* p. 16; Hopkins, *Lower Richland Planters,* p. 341; J.C. Hemphill, *Men of Mark in South Carolina* (Washington, D.C.: Men of Mark Publishing, 1909), vol. 4, p. 46; Janie M. Brooks to "Minnie," 10 March 1911 (Margaret Adams Gist Papers, South Caroliniana Library). Captain Brooks' war record was varied and distinguished, though he never attained high rank. From Dalton, Georgia on 30 April 1864 General Gist wrote presidential adviser Braxton Bragg recommending the Captain for promotion. Gist described Brooks as "my friend and Brother-in-law...a gallant, — efficient officer, and an educated Gentleman." States Rights Gist to Braxton Bragg, 30 April 1864 (States Rights Gist file, "Compiled Service Records").

6. Christie Zimmerman Fant, *The State House of South Carolina: An Illustrated Historic Guide* (Columbia: R.L. Bryan Co., 1970), p. 103.

Notes to Appendix One

1. Gee, *Gist family*, pp. 84-87.

2. Letter of Ellison Capers, 29 January 1880 (Ellison Capers Papers, South Caroliniana Library).

3. "States Rights Gist," *Garnet and Black*, 1902, p. 43. See note 26, chapter 10.

4. *Daily Courier*, 3 January 1865.

5. James T. Williams to David E. Finley, 21 October 1929 (David E. Finley Papers, South Caroliniana Library).

6. "States Rights Gist," *Garnet and Black*, 1902, p. 43.

7. Sam R. Watkins, *Co. Aytch, Maury Grays, First Tennessee Regiment*, reprint of 1882 edition (Jackson, Tennessee: McCowat-Mercer Press, 1952), pp. 127 and 220.

8. Charles, *Union County*, p. 198.

Notes to Appendix Two

1. This list has been compiled from information contained in the following sources: Joseph H. Crute, Jr., *Confederate Staff Officers, 1861-1865* (Powhatan, Virginia: Derwent Books, 1982), pp. 70-71; "Compiled Service Records of Confederate General and Staff Officers, and Non-Regimental Enlisted Men," National Archives; B.B. Smith to Ellison Capers, 19 July 1883 (Ellison Capers Collection, Citadel Archives); Hagood, *Memoirs;* General Order No. 1, 6 January 1863 (Thomas L. Clingman Papers, Southern Historical Collection).

Bibliography

MANUSCRIPTS

Benjamin Franklin Arthur Papers. South Caroliniana Library, University of South Carolina.

Ellison Capers Papers. William R. Perkins Library, Duke University.

Ellison Capers Collection. Citadel Archives, The Military College of South Carolina.

Ellison Capers Papers. South Caroliniana Library, University of South Carolina.

Thomas L. Clingman Papers. Southern Historical Collection, University of North Carolina.

"Compiled Service Records of Confederate General and Staff Officers, and Non-Regimental Enlisted Men." U.S. National Archives.

R.G.M. Dunovant Papers. William R. Perkins Library, Duke University.

John W. Ellis Papers. Southern Historical Collection, University of North Carolina.

David E. Finley Papers. South Caroliniana Library. University of South Carolina.

Margaret Adams Gist Papers. South Caroliniana Library, University of South Carolina.

States Rights Gist Papers. South Caroliniana Library, University of South Carolina.

George M. Hanvey Papers. Southern Historical Collection, University of North Carolina.

Theodore A. Honour Papers. South Caroliniana Library, University of South Carolina.

James Wilson Hudson Papers. South Caroliniana Library, University of South Carolina.

Joseph Brevard Kershaw Papers. South Caroliniana Library, University of South Carolina.

Richard Irvine Manning Papers. South Caroliniana Library, University of South Carolina.

George A. Mercer Papers. Southern Historical Collection, University of North Carolina.

William Porcher Miles Papers. Southern Historical Collection, University of North Carolina.

Records of the Union County Probate Court. South Carolina Department of Archives and History.

Records of the Union District Court of General Sessions. South Carolina Department of Archives and History.

James Hodge Saye Papers. South Caroliniana Library, University of South Carolina.

James Simons Papers. South Caroliniana Library, University of South Carolina.

South Carolina Engineer Bureau Records. South Caroliniana Library, University of South Carolina.

John Henry Steinmeyer, Jr. Papers. Southern Historical Collection, University of North Carolina.

Clement Hoffman Stevens Papers. South Caroliniana Library, University of South Carolina.

William H.T. Walker Papers. William R. Perkins Library, Duke University.

Thomas B. Walsh Papers. South Caroliniana Library, University of South Carolina.

Beaufort T. Watts Papers. South Caroliniana Library, University of South Carolina.

NEWSPAPERS

Charleston Courier, 1850.

Charleston Daily Courier, 1864-1865.

Charleston Mercury, 1831, 1850, 1861-1862.

Chester Standard, 1856.

Columbia *Daily Phoenix,* 1866.

Columbia *Daily South Carolinian,* 1864.

Columbia *Tri-Weekly Phoenix,* 1866.

Spartanburg *Carolina Spartan,* 1854, 1856-1858, 1860.

Unionville Journal, 1854-1855, 1858.

Yorkville Enquirer, 1855-1856, 1858-1859, 1861.

PRINTED RECORDS, JOURNALS, CATALOGS AND PAMPHLETS

Catalogue of the Regular and Honorary Members of the Clariosophic Socie-ty of the South Carolina College. Columbia: R.W. Gibbes, 1853.

Catalogue of the Trustees, Faculty and Students of the South Carolina Col-lege. Columbia: various printers, 1848-1851.

Cauthen, Charles E., ed. *Journals of the South Carolina Executive Coun-cils of 1861 and 1862.* Columbia: Archives Department, 1956.

Chesnut, James, Jr. *Report of the Chief of the Department of the Military of South Carolina to His Excellency Governor Pickens.* Columbia: Charles P. Pelham, 1862.

Harris, W.A., comp. *The Record of Fort Sumter From Its Occupation By Major Anderson to Its Reduction by South Carolina Troops.* Colum-bia: South Carolina Steam Job Printing Office, 1862.

Journal of the Congress of the Confederate States of America, 1861-1865. 7 volumes. Washington: Government Printing Office, 1904.

Journal of the Convention of the People of South Carolina. Charleston: Evans and Cogswell, 1861.

Journal of the House of Representatives of the State of South Carolina Be-ing the Sessions of 1860. Columbia: R.W. Gibbes, 1860.

Journal of the Senate of South Carolina. Columbia: State Printer, 1860-1861.

The Militia and Patrol Laws of South Carolina: To December, 1851. Columbia: Johnston and Cavis, 1852.

Minutes of the Military Commission at the Meeting in Greenville, South Carolina, August 4th 1859. Charleston: Evans and Co., 1859.

Quinquennial Catalog of the Law School of Harvard University, 1817-1934. Cambridge, Massachusetts: Published by the Law School, 1935.

Simons, James, *Address to the Officers of the Fourth Brigade Giving the Grounds of His Resignation.* Charleston: Evans and Cogswell, 1861.

Statutes at Large of South Carolina. Columbia: Republican Printing Co., 1874.

Sub-committee of the 1860 Association, G. Manigault, Chairman, *Suggestions As to the Arming of the State.* Charleston: Evans and Cogswell, 1860.

The Uniform of the Militia of South Carolina as Prescribed by the General Assembly at its Session of 1839. Columbia: A.H. Pemberton, 1840.

U.S. War Department, comp. *War of the Rebellion: A Compilation of the Official Records of the Union and Confederate Armies.* 128 volumes. Washington: Government Printing Office, 1880-1901.

Walker, C.I. "Historical Address." In *Ceremonies at the Unveiling of the South Carolina Monument on the Chickamauga Battlefield May 27th, 1901.* n.p., n.d.

ARTICLES

Dubose, William P. "Recollections of Mt. Zion School," *The Educational,* January 1903.

Eison, Ann Hames. "States Rights Gist," Charleston *News and Courier Sunday News,* 9 July 1922, part 2, p. 17.

Middleton, Susan. "Letters," *South Carolina Historical and Genealogical Magazine,* April 1963.

Miller's Planters' and Merchants' Almanac. Charleston: 1853.

Pettigrew, James J. "The Militia System of South Carolina," *Russell's Magazine,* March 1860, pp. 529-540.

Ramsdell, Charles W. "Lincoln and Fort Sumter," *The Journal of Southern History,* August 1937, pp. 259-288.

UNPUBLISHED MATERIAL

Bell, Daniel J. "Interpretive Booklets for Local Historic Sites: Rose Hill State Park, Union, S.C. as a Model." Unpublished Master's thesis, University of South Carolina, 1983.

Free, Lousarah Belle. "Education in Union County, South Carolina Prior to 1860." Unpublished Master's thesis, University of South Carolina, 1929.

BOOKS

Ball, William Watts. *The State That Forgot: South Carolina's Surrender to Democracy.* Indianapolis: Bobbs-Merrill Co., 1932.

Burton, E. Milby. *The Siege of Charleston 1861-1865.* Columbia: University of South Carolina Press, 1970.

Campbell, Thomas. *The Poetical Works.* London: Edward Moxon, 1837.

Capers, Walter B. *The Soldier-Bishop: Ellison Capers.* New York: Neale Publishing Co., 1912.

Carter III, Samuel. *The Siege of Atlanta, 1864.* New York: St. Martin's Press, 1973.

Cauthen, Charles E. *South Carolina Goes to War 1860-1865.* Chapel Hill, N.C.: University of North Carolina Press, 1950.

The Centennial History of the Harvard Law School, 1817-1917. n.p.: Harvard Law School Association, 1918.

Channing, Steven A. *Crisis of Fear: Secession in South Carolina.* New York: Simon & Schuster, 1970.

Charles, Allan D. *The Narrative History of Union County, S.C.* Spartanburg, S.C.: The Reprint Co., 1987.

Chesnut, Mary. *Mary Chesnut's Civil War.* Edited by C. Vann Woodward. New Haven: Yale University Press, 1981.

——————————. *The Private Mary Chesnut: The Unpublished Civil War Diaries.* Edited by C. Vann Woodward. New York: Oxford University Press, 1984.

Coit, Margaret L. *John C. Calhoun: American Portrait.* Boston: Houghton Mifflin Co., 1950.

Connelly, Thomas L. *Autumn of Glory: The Army of Tennessee, 1862-1865.* Baton Rouge: Louisiana State University Press, 1971.

Crute, Joseph H., Jr. *Confederate Staff Officers, 1861-1865.* Powhatan, Va.: Derwent Books, 1982.

Davis, William C. *Breckinridge: Statesman, Soldier, Symbol.* Baton Rouge: Louisiana State University Press, 1974.

de Tocqueville, Alexis. *Democracy in America.* Edited by J.P. Mayer. Translated by George Lawrence. Garden City, New York: Doubleday, 1969.

Dickert, Augustus. *History of Kershaw's Brigade.* Newberry, S.C.: Elbert H. Aull, Co., 1899.

Dorsey, Jean Muir, and Maxwell J. Dorsey. *Christopher Gist of Maryland and Some of His Descendants.* Chicago: John S. Swift Co., 1958.

Eliot, Samuel A. *A Sketch of the History of Harvard College and Its Present State.* Boston: Charles C. Little and James Brown, 1848.

Evans, Clement A., ed. *Confederate Military History.* 12 vols. Atlanta: Confederate Publishing, 1899.

Fant, Christie Zimmerman, *The State House of South Carolina: An Illustrated Historic Guide.* Columbia: R.L. Bryan Co., 1970.

Freeman, Douglas Southall. *Lee's Lieutenants: A Study in Command.* 3 vols. New York: Charles Scribner's Sons, 1942-1944.

_____. *Washington.* Abridgment by Richard Harwell. New York: Charles Scribner's Sons, 1968.

The Garnet and Black. Columbia: The South Carolina College, 1902.

Gee, Wilson. *The Gist Family of South Carolina and its Maryland Antecedents.* Charlottesville, Va.: Jarman's, Inc., 1934.

Gist, Margaret Adams, ed. *Presbyterian Women of South Carolina.* n.p.: Women's Auxiliary of the Synod of South Carolina, 1929.

Hagood, Johnson. *Memoirs of the War of Secession.* Columbia: The State Co., 1910.

Hamer, Philip M. *The Secession Movement in South Carolina, 1847-1852.* New York: Da Capo Press, 1971.

Hamilton, Alexander. "The Federalist No. 85." In *The Federalist*. Edited by Benjamin Fletcher Wright. Cambridge, Mass.: The Belknap Press of Harvard University Press, 1966.

Harper, William, et. al. *The Pro-Slavery Argument*. Philadelphia: Lippincott, Granbo & Co., 1853.

Hemphill, J.C. *Men of Mark in South Carolina*. 4 vols. Washington, D.C.: Men of Mark Publishing, 1909.

Hollis, Daniel Walker. *The University of South Carolina*. 2 vols. Columbia: University of South Carolina Press, 1951. Vol. 1: *South Carolina College*.

Hopkins, Laura J. *Lower Richland Planters: Hopkins, Adams, Weston and Related Families of South Carolina*. Columbia: Privately printed by R.L. Bryan Co., 1976.

Johnson, Allen, and Dumas Malone, eds. *Dictionary of American Biography*. New York: Charles Scribner's Sons, 1960.

Johnson, Robert Underwood, and Clarence Buel, eds. *Battles and Leaders of the Civil War*. 4 vols. New York: The Century Co., 1884-1887.

Kibler, Lillian Adele. *Benjamin F. Perry: South Carolina Unionist*. Durham, N.C.: Duke University Press, 1946.

King, Spencer Bidwell, Jr. *Ebb Tide, As Seen Through the Diary of Josephine Clay Habersham, 1863*. Athens, Ga.: University of Georgia Press, 1958.

LaBorde, Maximilian. *History of South Carolina College*. Charleston: Walker, Evans and Cogswell, 1874.

Lake, Will C. *Union County, Places and People*. Union, S.C.: Privately printed, 1982.

Losson, Christopher. *Tennessee's Forgotten Warriors: Frank Cheatham and His Confederate Division*. Knoxville: University of Tennessee Press, 1989.

Mabry, Mannie Lee, ed. *Union County Heritage*. Winston-Salem, N.C.: Hunter Publishing Co., 1981.

McBride, Robert M., and Dan M. Robison. *Biographical Dictionary of the Tennessee General Assembly*. 2 vols. Nashville: Tennessee Historical Commission, 1975.

McDonough, James Lee. *Chattanooga: A Death Grip on the Confederacy*. Knoxville: University of Tennessee Press, 1984.

_____, and Thomas L. Connelly. *Five Tragic Hours: The Battle of Franklin.* Knoxville: University of Tennessee Press, 1983.

McMaster, Fitz Hugh. *History of Fairfield County.* Columbia: State Commercial Printing Co., 1946.

McPherson, James M. *Battle Cry of Freedom: The Civil War Era.* New York: Oxford University Press, 1988.

Middleton, Margaret Simons. *Live Oak Plantation, Congaree, South Carolina.* Charleston: Nelson's Printing Co., 1956.

Mills, Robert. *Statistics of South Carolina.* Charleston: Hurlbut and Lloyd, 1826.

Morison, Samuel Eliot. *Three Centuries of Harvard: 1636-1936.* Cambridge, Mass.: The Belknap Press of Harvard University Press, 1936.

Nash, Howard P., Jr. *A Naval History of the Civil War.* New York: A.S. Barnes, 1972.

Nicolay, John G., and John Hay. *Abraham Lincoln: A History.* 10 vols. New York: The Century Co., 1917.

Nisbet, James Cooper. *Four Years on the Firing Line.* Edited by Bell Irvin Wiley. Jackson, Tenn.: McCowat-Mercer Press, 1963.

Oates, Stephen B. *To Purge This Land With Blood: A Biography of John Brown.* Amherst, Mass.: University of Massachusetts Press, 1984.

Palmer, B.M. *The Life and Letters of James Henley Thornwell, DD, LLD.* Richmond: Whittet and Shepperson, 1875.

Polk, William M. *Leonidas Polk: Bishop and General.* New York: Longmans, Green and Co., 1915.

Purdue, Howell, and Elizabeth Purdue. *Pat Cleburne: Confederate General.* Hillsboro, Texas: Hill Junior College Press, 1973.

Rivers, William James. *Rivers' Account of the Raising of Troops in South Carolina for State and Confederate Service 1861-1865.* Columbia: Bryan Printing, 1899.

Roman, Alfred. *The Military Operations of General Beauregard.* 2 vols. New York: Harper Brothers, 1884.

Rowland, Dunbar, ed. *Jefferson Davis, Constitutionalist: His Letters, Papers and Speeches.* 10 vols. Jackson, Miss.: Mississippi Department of Archives and History, 1923.

Ruchames, Louis, ed. *A John Brown Reader.* London: Abelard-Schuman, 1959.

Russell, William Howard. *My Diary North and South.* Boston: T.O.H.P. Burnham, 1863.

Scott, Otto J. *The Secret Six: John Brown and the Abolitionist Movement.* New York: Time Books, 1979.

Sherman, W.T. *Memoirs.* 2 vols. New York: Charles L. Webster, 1891.

Stephens, Alexander H. *A Constitutional View of the Late War Between the States.* 2 vols. Philadelphia: National Publishing Co., 1868.

Strode, Hudson. *Jefferson Davis: Confederate President.* New York: Harcourt, Brace and World, 1959.

Thomas, John P. *History of the South Carolina Military Academy.* Charleston: Walker, Evans and Cogswell, 1893.

Tilley, John Shipley. *Lincoln Takes Command.* Chapel Hill, N.C.: University of North Carolina Press, 1941.

[Tracy, Carlos]. "A Rebel Soldier's Diary of the Enemy's Approach to and Withdrawal From Before Charleston, S.C., May, June and July, 1862." In *Rebellion Record.* Edited by Frank Moore. 5 vols. New York: G.P. Putnam, 1862-1871.

Tucker, Glenn. *Chickamauga: Bloody Battle in the West.* Indianapolis: Bobbs-Merrill, 1961.

Warren, Charles. *History of the Harvard Law School.* New York: Da Capo Press, 1970.

Warren, Ezra J. *Generals in Blue.* Baton Rouge: Louisiana State University Press, 1964.

_____. *Generals in Gray.* Baton Rouge: Louisiana State University Press, 1959.

Watkins, Sam R. *Co. Aytch, Maury Grays, First Tennessee Regiment.* Reprint of 1882 edition. Jackson, Tenn.: McCowat-Mercer Press, 1952.

Williams, Jack K. "The Criminal Lawyer in Antebellum South Carolina." In *The Legal Profession: Major Historical Interpretations.* Edited by Kermit L. Hall. New York: Garland Publishing, 1987.

Williams, J.F. *Old and New Columbia.* Columbia: Epworth Orphanage Press, 1929.

Woodworth, Steven E. *Jefferson Davis and His Generals.* Lawrence, Kansas: University Press of Kansas, 1990.

Index

Abolitionism, 17, 18, 26, 41-42, 43-44
Adams, Caroline, 90
Adams, Ellen, 90
Adams, James Hopkins, 34, 35, 48, 73-74, 170n
Adams, Jane Margaret, 73
Adams, Jane Margaret ("Janie"), see Brooks, Jane Margaret
Adams, John, 143
Adams, Laura, 90, 148
Agassiz, Louis, 19
Aid, 54
Alabama Troops: 4th Infantry Regiment, 62, 63
Alexandria, Louisiana, 46
Alston, Robert Francis Withers, 36
Anderson, Colonel, 153
Anderson, Patton, 117
Anderson, Robert, 48-49, 51, 52, 53-54, 55, 57
Arthur, Benjamin Franklin, 28-29, 30, 74-75
Atlanta, 119, 125, 128-129, 130, 132, 133-134, 136-138
Augusta, Georgia, 91

Bartow, Francis S., 62
Bate, William B., 117, 127, 128, 129, 138, 141
Beauregard, Armand, 106
Beauregard, Pierre Gustave Toutant, 56-58, 62-63, 81-88, 89-90, 93, 141, 180n
Beauregard, René Toutant, 109, 111-112
Bee, Barnard Elliott, 62-63
Benham, Henry W., 79
Benjamin, Judah P., 65, 67
Boston, 17, 18, 23-25, 26-27
Bowie, J.A., 154
Bragg, Braxton, 95-96, 97-98, 100-101, 104, 105-106, 107-108, 110, 114-115, 182n
Branchville, South Carolina, 91

Brandon, Mississippi, 92-93
Breckinridge, John C., 43, 96, 101, 102, 106, 110, 112, 114
Brooks, Jane Margaret ("Janie"), 35, 73-74, 90-91, 115-116, 119, 140, 142, 143, 144, 146-148, 152, 179n
Brooks, John Hampden, 148, 182n
Brooks, Mary Adams, 90, 148
Brown, John, 41-42, 163n
Brown, John C., 134, 136, 138-139, 141
Brown, Joseph E., 45-46
Buchanan, James, 41, 49, 53
Buist, Henry, 42-43, 144
Butler, Lee M., 154

Calhoun, Georgia, 120
Calhoun, John C., 9, 18, 19, 21, 46, 58
Calhoun Station, Mississippi, 93
Cambridge, Massachusetts, 24, 25, 27
Campbell, Thomas, 7
Canton, Mississippi, 93
Capers, Ellison, 77, 79-80, 91, 95, 96, 100, 102, 116, 120, 121-122, 124, 130, 134-135, 136, 138, 141, 152, 180n
Carter, John, 143
Cassville, Georgia, 122
Castle Pinckney, South Carolina, 48, 49
Champion's Hill, Mississippi, 94
Chancellorsville, Virginia, 88
Charleston, South Carolina, 2, 4, 5, 38, 49-50, 51, 53-54, 56, 57, 58, 61, 77, 89, 90
Charleston Arsenal, 48-49, 50
Charleston Daily Courier, 143, 152
Charleston Mercury, 11, 72, 81, 171n
Chattanooga, 96, 105-112, 133
Cheatham, Benjamin F., 124, 128, 130, 132, 138-139, 140-141
Chesnut, James Jr., 61-62, 64, 66-68, 70, 74-75, 82, 144, 154
Chesnut, Mary, 64, 66, 70, 144
Chester District, South Carolina, 29
Choate, Joseph H., 26

Clariosophic Society, 19
Clay, Henry, 11
Cleburne, Patrick R., 101, 108-109, 110-111, 112-114, 119, 123, 124, 127, 129, 138, 143
Coles Island, South Carolina, 75, 77, 85
Colquitt, Peyton H., 89, 90, 92, 100, 102, 104
Columbia, South Carolina, 8, 15-16, 146-149
Columbia *Phoenix,* 148
Columbia *Telegraph,* 21
Columbia, Tennessee, 136
Compromise of 1850, 22, 25, 40
Confederate Memorial Day, 148
Conrad, Joseph, 142
Conscription, 68-69
Cooper, Thomas, 17, 38
Cooper, William, 154
Cromwell, Edith, 2-3
Cunningham, Charles, 7

Dalton, Georgia, 112, 115-120, 134, 182n
Davis, Jefferson, 55-56, 61-62, 66, 69-70, 72, 74-75, 81, 82, 98, 105-106, 115, 117, 119, 125, 132-134, 135, 177n
Dawkins, Thomas N., 31
Dearing, A.J., 154
Democratic Party, 41, 42, 43
Douglas, Stephen A., 43
DuBose, William Porcher, 15
Dunovant, John, 154
Dunovant, Robert Gill Mills, 35, 52-53, 55
Dupont, Samuel F., 86

Early, Jubal Anderson, 64
Ector, Matthew, 102, 104
Edwards, Oliver Evans, 32, 34
1860 Association, 50
Ellet, William, 17
Ellis, John W., 45, 163n
Emerson, Ralph Waldo, 25
Euphradian Society, 19
Evans, Doctor, 101
Evans, Nathan George, 78, 79-80, 88, 171n

Fair Forest Presbyterian Church, 12
Ferguson, T.B., 89, 98
Forest Station, Mississippi, 93
Forrest, Nathan Bedford, 138, 139-140
Fort Johnson, South Carolina, 54, 57, 86
Fort Moultrie, South Carolina, 48-50, 54, 55, 57, 75
Fort Sumter, South Carolina, 24, 48-49, 50, 51, 52, 53-54, 55-58, 60, 75, 86
Franklin, Tennessee, 138-143, 155n
Freeman, Douglas Southall, 3
French, Samuel, 123

Garden, Henry DeSaussure, 141, 154, 181
Garrison, William Lloyd, 18, 25
General Clinch, 49
Georgetown, South Carolina, 75
Georgia Troops:
1st Battalion Georgia Sharpshooters, 122; 2nd Battalion Georgia Sharpshooters, 126; 8th Georgia Battalion, 89, 90, 98, 122; 39th Georgia Regiment, 109; 46th Georgia Regiment, 89, 90, 98, 104, 122; 65th Georgia Regiment, 126
"Gertrude of Wyoming" (poem), 7, 27, 160n
Gettysburg, 95, 114
Gist, Christopher (Gist ancestor), 2-3
Gist, Christopher (explorer), 3
Gist, Elizabeth Lewis McDaniel, 5, 11, 12, 42, 66
Gist, Francis, 4, 38
Gist, Independent, 4
Gist, James Dugan, 12, 74, 90, 95, 155, 160n
Gist, Jane Margaret ("Janie"), see Brooks, Jane Margaret
Gist, John (cousin), 12
Gist, John Cornelius (brother), 12
Gist, Joseph (uncle), 38
Gist, Joseph Fincher (brother), 12, 16, 30, 38, 73, 104, 148
Gist, Louisa Sarah, 157n
Gist, Mary, 27
Gist, Mordecai, 4
Gist, Nathaniel (Indian trader), 3
Gist, Nathaniel (father), 4-7, 8, 9, 10, 11, 12-13, 20, 22, 38, 58-59, 66, 72, 73
Gist, Nathaniel (brother), 1-2, 12, 27
Gist, Richard, 3
Gist, Robert Thaddeus, 12, 160n
Gist, Sarah Fincher (grandmother), 3, 4
Gist, Sarah Frances (sister), 2, 12
Gist, States, 4
Gist, States Rights:
ancestry, 2-8; birth, 11; events that influenced his naming, 9-12; boyhood, 12-13; early education, 12-15; at South Carolina College, 15-18, 19-21; at Harvard Law School, 22-28; Captain of Johnson Rifles, 30-31, 33-34; governor's aide-de-camp, 34, 42; Brigadier General of militia, 34-37, 42-43; secretary and adviser to Governor Gist, 42-43, 164n; diplomatic mission, 44-47, 163n; appointed Adjutant and Inspector General, 52, 165n; Fort Sumter bombardment, 52-53, 54-58; mobilization work, 60-62, 64-69; Manassas, 61-64; elected Adjutant and Inspector General, 66; commissioned Confederate Brigadier

General, 69-72, 74-75; Secessionville, 75-80, 86; service on South
Carolina coast, 72, 74, 75, 77-88;
commands in North Carolina, 83-84,
85-86; marriage, 90-91; commands
division sent West, 89-94; service in
Mississippi,*87, 91-96;
Chickamauga, 98-105, 175n; siege
of Chattanooga, 104-108; Missionary
Ridge, 108-114; Dalton, 115-120,
182n; Atlanta campaign, 119-131;
Resaca, 120-121; Kennesaw Mountain, 123-125, 126; Peachtree Creek,
126-127; Battle of Atlanta, 127-128;
Jonesboro, 129-130; Tennessee
campaign, 133-142, 180n; Spring
Hill, 138-139; Franklin, 1-2,
139-142, 152-153; death and burial,
141-143, 152-153; Columbia funeral,
146-147, 182n; criticized, 85-86, 87,
172n; estate, 148; horses, 109, 130,
139, 140, 141, 148, 153; misspellings of name, 182n; political views,
21, 31; praised, 21, 28, 31, 33-34,
42, 47, 56, 63, 66, 70, 72, 80, 84,
104-105, 106, 114, 116-117,
144-145, 153; staff, 74, 83, 128,
141, 142, 152-153, 154-155,181n
Gist, Thomas McDaniel, 12
Gist, William (grandfather), 2-4, 5
Gist, William Crawford (brother), 12
Gist, William Henry (cousin), 16, 38-40,
42-43, 44-47, 48, 49, 60, 67, 73,
164n
Glenn, John B., 13
Glenn Springs, South Carolina, 35
Glover, Joseph, 155
Gordon, George, 141
Granbury, Hiram, 143
Grant, Ulysses S., 92-93, 94-95, 105,
106-107, 110, 134, 135
Green, John S., 155
Greenville, South Carolina, 22, 144-145
Greenville Southern Patriot, 22
Gregg, Maxcy, 51
Gwynn, Walter, 55

Habersham, Joseph Clay, 128, 155
Hagood, Johnson, 78, 82, 88, 90, 155
Hamilton, Alexander, 10
Hampton, Wade, 63
Hardee, William J., 106, 111, 112-114,
115, 126-127, 128, 129-130,
133-134, 180n
Harlee, William Wallace, 67, 74-75
Harper's Ferry, 41-42
Harper, William, 19
Harrise, Henri, 15
Harris, Isham G., 117, 177n
Harrow, William, 130, 179n
Harvard Law School, 23, 25-26, 27,
160n
Hayne, Isaac William, 67

Helm, Benjamin Hardin, 101
Henry, Robert, 17
Hill, Daniel Harvey, 97, 101-102
Hindman, Thomas Carmichael, 97
Honour, Theodore A., 172n
Hood, John Bell, 122-123, 125-140,
143, 146
Hooker, Joseph, 106-107, 112, 127
Houston, Sam, 45
Howard, Wiley, 72, 130, 139, 140-143,
145, 152, 179n, 180n
Hudson, Jacob W., 14-15, 20
Hunt, J.M., 155

Jackson, Andrew, 11, 19
Jackson, Mississippi, 92-93, 95
Jackson, Thomas Jonathan, 63, 148
Jamison, David F., 54
Johnston, Joseph E., 62, 63, 92-95,
115-116, 117, 119, 120-125,
132-133
Jonesboro, Georgia, 129-130, 136
Jones, James, 74-75, 170n

Kennesaw Mountain, Georgia,
123-125, 126
Keokuk, 86
Kershaw, Joseph B., 57
King, Mallory P., 155
Kings Mountain, South Carolina, 3
Kingston, Georgia, 98, 100
Knoxville, 106

LaBorde, Maximilian, 17
Lamar, Thomas G., 78-79
Langdell, Christopher Columbus, 26
Lee, Robert E., 41, 65-66, 68, 72, 77,
85, 87, 88, 96, 114, 135
Lee, Stephen D., 139
Liddell, St. John R., 102, 104-105,
175n
Lieber, Francis, 17
Lincoln, Abraham, 43-44, 45, 46-47,
56-57, 58, 61, 69, 105
"Live Oak" (plantation), 73, 90, 143,
146
Longstreet, James, 96, 100, 103, 106
Lovejoy's Station, Georgia, 130-131

McCullough, James, 89, 120, 128,
129
McDowell, Irvin, 61, 62
McKinzie, W.G., 155
McLaws, LaFayette, 155
McPherson, James B., 120, 127
Magrath, Andrew G., 54
Maney, George Earl, 109, 112, 127,
129
Marietta, Georgia, 125
Marion, 54
Marion Rifles Glee Club, 91
Maturin, Edward, 15

"Maum Mary" (Mary Chesnut's servant), 72
Means, Hugh, 5
Melton, Samuel W., 36, 162n
Mercer, Hugh W., 78
Middleton, Susan, 172n
Miles, William Porcher, 70, 170n
Mississippi Troops:
    2nd Mississippi Regiment, 62; 5th Mississippi Regiment, 126, 128; 8th Mississippi Regiment, 126, 128; 11th Mississippi Regiment, 62
Montgomery, Alabama, 55-56, 57, 92
Moore, Andrew Barry, 46
Moore, Thomas O., 46
Morton, Mississippi, 95, 155n
Mount Zion Institute, 13, 14-15, 20
Munro, William, 160n

Nance, William F., 155
Nashville, 22, 135, 138, 140, 143, 146, 154n
New Bern, North Carolina, 83
Newman Guards, 164n
New York *Tribune*, 77
Nina, 49
Nisbet, James C., 107, 109, 111-112, 127
Nullification, 9-12

Ogier, Thomas L., 95

Palmetto, Georgia, 132-134
Palmetto State, 81
Parker, Joel, 26, 27, 28
Parsons, Theophilus, 26
Pemberton, John C., 72, 74, 75-77, 78, 79-80, 81, 85, 87, 89, 91-92, 94
Perry, Benjamin F., 47, 69, 144-145, 164n
Perry, M.S., 46
Petersburg, Virginia, 83
Pettus, John J., 46
Pickens, Francis W., 49, 52, 53-58, 60-61, 65, 67, 81, 82, 106, 165n
Pocataligo, 82, 87
Polk, Leonidas, 97, 102, 103, 105, 123
Port Royal, South Carolina, 65
Preston, William Campbell, 16

Republican Party, 31, 42, 43-46
Resaca, Georgia, 120-121
Revolutionary War, 2, 3-4, 7
Reynolds, Alexander, 126
Rice, Elliott, W., 121
Richland District, South Carolina, 73
Richmond, 61-62, 64, 83
Ringgold, Georgia, 98, 100, 112, 114
Ripley, Roswell, S., 56, 82, 85-86, 87, 155
Rome, Georgia, 96, 98
Rosecrans, William S., 96, 97, 101, 102-104, 105

"Rose Hill" (plantation), 38
Rough and Ready, Georgia, 129
Russell, William, 58

Savannah, 65, 78
Savannah, 61
Saye, James Hodge, 12-13, 66
Secession, 19-20, 21-22, 25, 31, 40, 41-42, 43-47, 50, 51-52, 58-59, 69, 164n
Secessionville, South Carolina, 75, 77-80, 87
Seddon, James A., 94
Sequoyah (George Gist), 3
Schofield, John M., 126, 135, 138, 139, 140
Screven, Thomas E., 20, 21
Sherman, William Tecumseh, 94-95, 106-107, 109-111, 119, 120-130, 132-133, 134-135, 136-138, 146
Simons, James, 42, 51, 52-53, 60-61
Simonton, Charles H., 61, 64, 106
Slaves and slavery, 8, 18-19, 21, 22, 25, 26, 32, 119, 170n
Smith, B.B., 155
Smith, Gustavus Woodson, 84
Smith, R.B., 155
Smith, William Duncan, 78, 79-80, 154, 155
South Carolina College, 13, 14, 15-18, 19-21, 27, 38
South Carolina Corps of Engineers, 51, 55
South Carolina Executive Council, 54, 67-69, 70, 74-75, 77, 82
South Carolina Military Academy, 53-54, 74, 154
South Carolina Militia, 41, 49, 51, 52, 68, 161n; criticism of, 31-33, 35-36, 50; organization, 30-32, 34
South Carolina Ordnance Bureau, 51, 52
South Carolina Regular Army, 51, 53
South Carolina Troops:
    1st South Carolina Regiment, 51-52; 15th South Carolina Regiment, 104; 16th South Carolina Regiment, 89, 98, 120, 122, 128, 155; 24th South Carolina Regiment, 89, 90, 91, 98, 120, 122, 124, 132-133, 134-135, 141, 155, 181n
South Carolina Volunteer Forces, 50-51
Sparks, Jared, 27
Spartanburg, South Carolina, 35, 36
Spartanburg *Carolina Spartan*, 35
Spartanburg District, South Carolina, 29, 35
Spring Hill, Tennessee, 138-139
Stanley, David, 135
Star of the West, 53-54
States' rights, 9-12, 19-20, 40, 51, 58-59
Steinmeyer, John, 109

Stephens, Alexander, 10
Stevens, Clement Hoffman, 89, 100, 102, 116, 122
Stevenson, Carter L., 108, 109
Stewart, Alexander P., 134, 139, 140-141
Stowe, Harriet Beecher, 27
Strahl, Otho, 138, 143
Sumner, Charles, 25
Sweeny, Thomas W., 120-121

Tallahassee, Florida, 46
Tariff, 9, 11-12, 41
Thomas, George H., 103, 105, 106-107, 111, 126, 135, 138
Thompson, Andrew McBride, 5
Thornwell, James H., 17-18, 27
Tillman, James A., 132-133
Tocqueville, Alexis de, 19
Tracy, Carlos, 74, 155
Trapier, James H., 86
Trenholm, Frank, 141-142, 152-153, 155
Trinity Episcopal Church, Columbia, South Carolina, 146-148
Turchin, John, 103-104, 175n
Turner, Nat, 18
Tyler, John, 56

***Uncle Tom's Cabin*, 26-27**
Union District, South Carolina, 2, 4-5, 8, 11, 22, 40
Unionville, South Carolina, 23-24, 28-29, 45, 148, 163n
Unionville Female Academy, 162n
Unionville Journal, 28, 31

Vicksburg, 87, 92, 94, 95

Walker, Joseph, 74, 155
Walker, Leroy P., 61
Walker, William Henry Talbot, 89-90, 93-94, 96, 102, 104-105, 108, 115-116, 119, 120-122, 125, 126, 127, 128
Washington, George, 3, 19
Watkins, Sam, 153
Watters, Z.L., 89
Watts, Beaufort T., 42, 45
Whitehead, Doctor, 95
White, Mrs. William, 143
Whiting, William Henry Chase, 56, 82-84
Whitney, Eli, 8
Williams, James H., 34, 35
Williams, James T., 153
Wilmington, North Carolina, 83-84, 91
Wilmot, David, 21
Wilson, Claudius, 102, 104
Winchester, Virginia, 62
Winnsboro, South Carolina, 13-14
Wood, Thomas J., 103
Wright, Doctor, 142, 143
Wright, John, 12
"Wyoming" (plantation), 7-8, 9, 12, 13, 23, 27, 58, 66, 72, 73, 95, 157n

Yazoo City, Mississippi, 93
York District, South Carolina, 29
Yorkville Enquirer, 32, 35-37, 42